Before the Greeks

Before the Greeks

M. Chahin

The Lutterworth Press
Cambridge

The Lutterworth Press
P.O. Box 60
Cambridge
CB1 2NT

British Library Cataloguing in Publication Data:
A catalogue record is available from the British Library.

ISBN 0 7188 2950 6

Printed in Great Britain by Hillman Printers
(Frome) Ltd.

To my daughter Myra

Contents

List of Illustrations

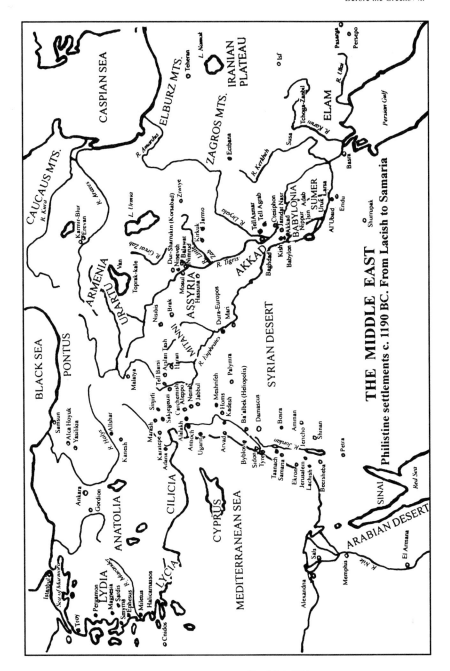

THE MIDDLE EAST
Philistine settlements c. 1190 BC. From Lachish to Samaria

PREFACE

This work is in memory of my friend and mentor, the late Cecil Gubbin of Richmond, Surrey, who, long ago, introduced me to the absorbing subject of the ancient history of the Near East where, most scholars now agree, the foundations of Western Civilization are to be found. Its historical breadth, which could be described as an introduction to classical studies, should stimulate the interest of the general reader of history.

I wish to record gratefully the generous support I received in my academic activities over a period of many years, from the late Professor David M. Lang of the School of Oriental and African Studies, University of London. I am pleased to express my sincere thanks to Graham C. L. Berthon for patiently reading the manuscript at its early stage and offering his valued comments.

I remember with pleasure the audiences who regularly attended my lectures on aspects of the ancient history of the Near East at colleges in London , at the Richmond, Surrey, Adult College and, in more recent years, in the West Country under the auspices of the Universities of Bristol and Exeter. I am happy to acknowledge the courtesy of the authorities of the London and Richmond institutes and those of the two universities.

I wish to record gratefully the assistance courteously given to me by the Photographic Service of the Trustees of the British Museum. My thanks are offered to the authors and publishers of my indispensable sources.

Chapter 1
The Background

This book is a brief introduction to the ancient history of the Near East. Its purpose is to demonstrate the immense cultural debt of the Classical Greeks, the Romans and western civilization as a whole, to the peoples who lived in the Near East for thousands of years before them.

Of particular importance is the geographical area described as 'Mesopotamia' or the land between the rivers Euphrates (about 1,700 miles) Tigris (about 1,150 miles). On emerging from their sources in the Caucasus and the highlands of Armenia they negotiate the steep drop onto the plains of Mesopotamia and flow rapidly southward in nearly parallel courses eventually joining to form a long, common channel called Shat el Arab, which empties into the Persian Gulf. To the east of that region are the Zagros mountains, to the west lies the Syrian desert. A tributary from the west flowing into Shat el Arab is now a wadi, but from the east the Karun is still in full flow. These rivers, especially those from the north, carried large quantities of silt into what was once the northern arm of the Persian Gulf. The silt created a bar and eventually a lagoon of fresh water opening out into a delta. Increasing amounts of silt flowing into the lagoon raised its bed and created dry land. The whole of that ancient region of Mesopotamia is often described as 'Babylonia'.

It is near the junction of the two rivers, in south Babylonia, in the land of Sumer (the Biblical Shinar (Genesis X.10)), that the sites of the most ancient cities are to be found, such as Uruk or Warka (the Biblical Erech (Gen. X.10)) where writing was first developed and Ur 'of the Chaldees' (the city associated with Abraham (Gen.XI.28)); the holy city of Nippur and the royal city of Eridu. Further north, the ancient site of Babylon on the Euphrates is nearly opposite modern Baghdad on the river Tigris, separated by only about 30 miles of a fertile and shaded oasis, perhaps the site of the Garden of Eden, for the native name of that narrow neck of land is Edin.

Far to the west of Sumer, beyond the Syrian desert, stretched the wilderness of Palestine and Syria, where the valleys of the rivers Jordan and Orontes were used by nomads on their travels. A short crossing at the apex of the Fertile Crescent would have lead them to the north-south course of the Euphrates. In the north, at the eastern end of the mountainous Asia Minor, rise the 'mountains of Ararat'

Figure 1. Portrait head of the pre-pottery Neolithic phase, Jericho. The features were modelled in plaster on the actual skull. After K. M. Kenyon, from Sonia Cole, The Neolithic Revolution. *Courtesy, Trustees of the British Museum.*

(Gen.VIII.4), the southern foothills of the Caucasus. The western end of the east-west valleys of Anatolia[1] is the Mediterranean coast where the Ionian city states appeared (c.1200). From the many inlets of that coast small boats could cross over to the Greek mainland via the safety of the 'stepping stones' of the Cyclades, thus establishing communications between Asia and Europe. Soon, from the great ports on the Syria-Palestine coast bold traders would sail to Cyprus, Crete, Egypt, Greece and beyond.

Early communities and social organisations are full of taboos and restrictive rules of behaviour, which are inherited and imposed upon the people by mighty chiefs and awesome priests. As social and political institutions became increasingly stable, the power of governing individuals increased. Such powers were delegated with increasing confidence and safety, and restrictions on the movements and self expression of individuals were gradually relaxed. So the development of craft-skills was encouraged, in tandem with the complications of increasingly sophisticated conventions of trading and commercial activities. In short, the initial and necessary disciplines for the development of the social and political institutions of communities were progressively relaxed and the mores and habits of civilization with all its complexities were gradually established.

Freedom is possible only within a framework. At first the two expressions – freedom and framework – seem to be mutually exclusive. But an example might be enough to explain the implication of that principle: a river would cease to be a river if its waters were not restricted by its two banks – it would be a watery chaos; the existence of a community describes the interdependence and integrity of its members – each behaving within the restrictions imposed upon and accepted by the whole. The laws themselves are adapted to the requirements of an evolving community.

The meaning of civilization is concerned with cities. The immense time span of hundreds of thousands of years which embody the Old and the New Stone Ages came to an end about 12,000 years ago, soon after the discovery of wheat

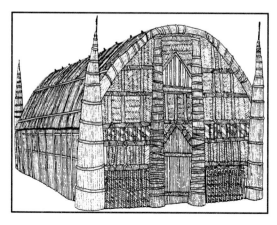

Figure 2. Hut made of marsh reeds, c. 3400 BC. The same form of construction is still used by marsh Arabs today.

in the wild which, crossed with a natural grass, formed a fertile hybrid. It could then be planted and reaped annually. The domestication of animals for their various uses – milk, skin, bone, transport – the tools and skills in carving wood and hewing stone to required shapes and the moulding of mudclay into building bricks, encouraged, indeed demanded, permanent settlements near rivers where hamlets, villages and towns arose. Such settlements imply division of labour. That is not possible without a surplus of corn and agricultural products to feed urban populations. The massive stone walls of a settlement close to a spring, discovered on the site of Jericho, is an astonishing architectural feat at the end of the Neolithic period, about 9,000 years ago. It would have been an impressive architectural achievement at any period.

> Around it on the outside ran a rock-cut ditch 8 meters wide and more than 2 meters deep and at one point, where it still stands to a height of almost a meter, it was backed by a massive circular tower. The tower, which was also solidly built of stone, is preserved to a height of 9 meters with a diameter of about 9 meters at the top. The summit was reached by an internal stair of 28 steps, each a single block of stone more than a meter wide, that was approached from the settlement inside the wall.[2]

This was discovered in 1936 by Prof. John Garstang,[3] and explored by Dr. Kathleen Kenyon in 1951.[4] Such massive stone walls with a tower, could only have been for defensive purpose; they show unexpected architectural advances. The sites of other cities of about the same period in central Anatolia such as Catal Hüyük, have been described by a number of archaeologists.

> The Neolithic civilization revealed at Catal Hüyük [a settlement three times larger than that at Jericho], shines like a supernova among the rather dim galaxy of contemporary peasant cultures. The comparison is apt, for Catal Hüyük burnt itself out and left no permanent mark on the cultural development of Anatolia after c.5000 BC. A faint afterglow may be detected in the Halaf culture of North Mesopotamia, but this, too, was doomed to disappear. Its most lasting effect was not felt in the Near East, but in Europe, for it was to this new continent that the Neolithic cultures of Anatolia introduced the first beginnings of agriculture and stock-breeding and the cult of the Mother Goddess, the basis of our civilization.[5]

The two towns were only 500 miles apart. There must have been communications between them. Clay, available in abundance, could be shaped into figurines of gods and goddesses, as well as domestic implements. Its soft surface also encouraged graphic experiments – drawings which carried a message, such as the contents of a pot. The best examples, some beautifully painted and even slightly glazed pottery, dated to about 5000 BC, were found in northern Mesopotamia, in the vicinity of modern Mosul, the centre of the Tell Halaf Pottery Culture. The Halaf cultural region included the volcanic mountains of central and eastern Anatolia, whence the important trade in obsidian (a volcanic stone) would also have been controlled.

An inferior pottery culture, the al'Ubaid material (c.4900), first discovered near Ur, then at Eridu and Erech influenced much of Mesopotamia. Distinguished by a well made buff pottery. 'Ubaid with its skills in manipulating clay into sickles and domestic ware, shaping figurines of domesticated animals, making whorls of bitumen or baked clay for spinning woollen thread, obliterated Halaf amidst destruction and massacre. Ubaid settlers began a new era in which the foundations of Sumerian civilization were established. They learnt that seasonal floods laid a blanket of silt which enriched the fertility of the soil. Their principal crop was barley which provided food for man and beast. Wheat was also cultivated, but in smaller quantities, barley being the hardier seed. Fruit trees were planted and the wood of old trunks and their boughs provided much needed timber in a land of only frail trees – palm, poplar and willow, none of them strong enough for large buildings. Marsh reeds were used by the poorer people for constructing huts in which they lived, as do the poorer Arab peasantry today. They soon discovered that timber of larger trees could be obtained from the foothills of the nearby Zagros mountains for buildings of the wealthier members of the social hierarchy.

The Ubaid or Sumerian civilization quickly spread from the lower reaches of the two rivers, from Eridu and Uruk (Warka or Erech), northwards along the river valleys, to Babylon and beyond. Its survival and prosperity depended entirely on the widespread use of irrigation with the abundant waters of the rivers, which could be diverted by a system of canals extensively built and developed with sluices and dikes. Their importance is demonstrated by the presence of official inspectors to supervise their upkeep. Agriculture developed apace, and the crafts prospered. In time, food production was so efficiently organised that Mesopotamia became the granary of the Near East. Good communications between cities and their inhabitants were provided by the waterways and hard paths between towns, which encouraged trade and the incidental, but very important, exchange of ideas.

The first literate Sumerians seem to have emerged more than 5000 years ago, from Uruk which covered about 170 acres, with a population of perhaps well over 20,000. The most striking demonstration of the great changes in the way of life of those early people, following the satisfactory organisation of food supplies, was writing, the catalyst which made the difference between primitive and sophisticated societies. The Sumerians, who are introduced in chapter 2, were the people who developed primitive pictographs into an alphabetic writing. An advanced social structure would not have been possible without written laws, and instructions. We do not know the reasons for the disappearance of the highly advanced stone age civilization of Jericho, to which I referred earlier – like the snuffing out of a used-up candle. Perhaps it was because of the absence of the powerful adhesive, writing, which binds together social institutions and the historical inheritance of a community into a continuous, unbreakable whole.

The historical span of this book is about 6,000 years, down to the end of the Persian Empire, destroyed by Alexander the Great in 331. To cover that period, we shall touch upon several peoples and places both adjacent to and well beyond Mesopotamia, such as Egypt and Crete. That vast region, the many centuries and the peoples involved, will be reviewed quickly because this is only a brief outline of the ancient history of the Near East. The book is concieved as two historical periods: (a) the histories of events approximately between 3000 BC and 1200 BC, the Bronze Age, merging into (b) the histories of the peoples who emerged around the end of the thirteenth century BC at about the times of the Iron Age (when iron became commonplace), a great historical watershed, a time of upheavals in the political geography of the Near East. The people of Sumer, Akkad, Babylon and Assyria, each learning from its predecessors, in turn produced a distinctive civilization, culminating in the indispensable intellectual and material achievements of Classical Greece, which were adopted by Rome and introduced into Western Europe. The emergence of Classical Greece, therefore, represents the marvellous apogee of millennia of social and political development in the Near East. Yet, Sir Moses Finley, in analysing Periclean Greece, declared that

> British scholars had for long sentimentalised Athens. They attributed modern notions of liberty and Democracy to a society that was imperialist and rested on slavery. We should accept that, far from handing down to us eternal truths, Greece and Rome were totally 'other' - as unlike our own culture as that of an African tribe or Polenisian islanders.[9]

I do not necessarily agree with all of the learned writer's highly interesting comment. But the controversial statement introduces an unusual aspect of history, which should be studied.

Notes

1. The strictly geographical term, 'Anatolia' defines the region in modern Turkey, from the west of the Euphrates, before it enters Syria, to the Mediterranean; it is also called 'Asia minor'. But the term 'Anatolia' is often used (as in this book) for the whole of modern Turkey.
2. Oates David and Joan, *The Rise of Civilisation*, Phaidon, Oxford, 1976, p.76,
3. Garstang John, *The Story of Jericho*, London, 1940.
4. Kenyon Kathleen M., *Digging up Jericho*, London, 1960-65.
5. Mellaart James, *Earliest Civilizations of the Near East*, London, 1963, p.77
6. Burney Charles, *From Village to Empire*, Phaidon, Oxford, 1977, p.76
7. Lloyd Seton, *Ancient Turkey*, Guild Publishing, London, 1989
8. Burney Charles and Lang David Marshall, *The Peoples of the Hills*, Weidenfeld & Nicolson, London 1971.
9. Annan Noel, *Our Age*, London, 1990, p. 358

For more detailed and recent information on Anatolia and Mesopotamia (for the chapters throughout this book), the reader may refer to The Cambridge Ancient History, volumes I - IV (consult the indexes) and the professional archaeological journals, Anatolian Studies and Iraq, published annually, by the British School of Archaeology (University of London). Relevant and highly interesting articles will also be found in The Journal of the Royal Asiatic Society, London (consult its indexes, obtainable separately).

Chapter 2
Sumer

The Babylonian Creation story tells that Marduk, the god of gods, vanquished the Great Mother Goddess, Tiamat, deity of the primeval watery spirit of Chaos, represented by the marshlands of the Euphrates and the Tigris, before they emptied into the Gulf. He laid a reed upon the water and by pouring dust upon it, formed the first land. Thus, Marduk created the earth, and he was well pleased. It was then possible to make bricks; houses and cities arose; Uruk, the royal city of Eridu and the holy city of Nippur were built and peopled, 'in the land of Shinar' (Gen.X.10) or Sumer.

Why start at Sumer? Do I agree with Archbishop James Ussher who in 1654, after much mathematical gymnastics, based upon the Book of Genesis, concluded that the world was created on 4 October, 4004 BC? It must be admitted that it was a good guess! Sumer, a collection of city-states in southern Mesopotamia, such as Ur, Uruk, Eridu and Nippur gradually appeared on the historical scene out of the Ubaid culture (see chapter 1). The Sumerians eventually built upon it their sophisticated civilization. Most importantly, they invented and developed a vehicle – writing – whereby events, ideas and information could be recorded and transmitted. Sumer was, therefore, the first literate society.

The origin of the Sumerians is still a matter for discussion amongst scholars – it is not yet known. Their language does not reflect any known group of languages and it is described as 'agglutinative'. Sculptures show them with large, bulging eyes, shaven heads and curly beards. Also, thousands of tablets, many stelae and monuments describe their civic and private activities in detail. It is the oldest known literary language; it influenced the West far more than Egypt.

Agriculture was the foundation of the Mesopotamian economy. Although the natural face of Mesopotamia was a desert, the abundant waters of the great rivers were directed into well maintained canals, reaching out far beyond the river banks, to water the corn fields and enrich them with deposits of silt. Irrigation techniques improved, a simple wooden plough was devised, this type is still used in the Near East today, and the fertile plain produced more than enough for an increasing population. The produce of the land was seasonally gathered, stored and distributed by the temple which was also the warehouse for the surplus farm products. Sir Mortimer Wheeler gives some interesting

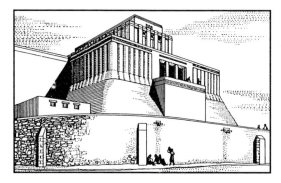

Figure 3. Reconstruction of the temple at Eridu. Predynastic period (c. 3200 BC). The oldest Sumerian religious structure has been found at Eridu.

statistics regarding the quantities and storage of grain in Ur (as in other cities of Mesopotamia during the same period). In the Tigris-Euphrates Valley all the important cities possessed granaries, often of considerable size. Some were attached to temples, others were situated on the banks of canals . . . or dispersed in other parts of the cities. A text from Ur implies that one of the granaries stored enough barley to provide wages for 4,020 days; another text refers to the commandant of the granary who was responsible for seeing that 10,930 man-days' payment was made out of his store, presumably in barley, to meet the wages of workers from the town; the workers included scribes, overseers, shepherds and irrigators. Another text refers to royal barley, to be returned with interest, received by Lulamu from the granary of the canal-bank. All these documents are of c.2130-2000 BC. [1]

Crops as well as sheep, cattle and other domesticated animals gradually created a complex farming economy. The enormous surplus harvest of grain and other food products, which were stored in the temple warehouse, made the division of labour possible and resulted in a social structure. Craftsmen, for example, did not have to concern themselves with farming. They could specialise in their skills and in return for their wares they received their food. The farm livestock was properly cared for and its various services were used for the community; the craftsmen who could rise to be architects and engineers were an essential part of the social hierarchy. They were responsible for the construction of canals, sluices and public buildings. Roads had evolved by the middle of the third millennium from 'straightened paths' to essential links of communication with the world outside the city.

Craftsmanship (including architecture) was an ancient inheritance. At first the unlimited quantity of clay gave humble workers ample opportunities for experimenting and for devising pots, jars and other necessary domestic utensils, as well as agricultural tools. Buildings were constructed of bricks made of mud-clay, mixed with straw or grit, and baked clay for building-bricks (known as 'terracotta' in art); sun-dried ('unburnt' or 'adobe') bricks (any shape) for other purposes. Stones for buildings had to be imported on rafts down river from Anatolia or from the neighbouring Zagros mountains. The arch was invented. The principle of the fulcrum and lever were understood from their forefathers, as were the water (our spirit) level and plumb line. 'Craftsmen' were also fine architects; the designs of their temples and palaces dominating the cities on high ground, such as those at Eridu and Tepe Gawra, are quite modern in conception, with simple lines and, most surprisingly, they even knew how to apply the principle of entasis to correct optical illusion. The walls of a house at Tepe Gawra seem to have been decorated with paintings in red and black.

Metal is very rare in the south. Cast axes of copper discovered in the north, indicate important advances in metallurgy. A very fine copper model of a bull, of Sumerian origin (c.2300 BC) was discovered near Lake Van, and is now exhibited at the British Museum. Metal workers mastered the technique of casting bronze c.3100, which results from a mixture of copper with about eight per cent of tin. Copper and tin were obtainable from central and eastern Anatolia. Silver and, at the end of that period, gold were obtainable from south-west Anatolia, although gold dust was imported earlier from eastern Anatolia by Gudea, governor of Lagash (c.2190). There were mirrors and ornamental articles made of obsidian, imported from the volcanic regions of Mount Ararat and the Amanus mountains. Craftsmen expressed their artistic aspirations very successfully: stone beads and cowries and dentalium from the Gulf were fashioned into bracelets, rings and necklaces; drawings of domestic scenes traced upon a variety of semi-precious stone seals, such as steatite (soap-stone), diorite, carnelian, haematite and lapis lazuli found at Tepe Gawra[2] were formed into adornments of beautiful jewellery for prestigious, religious or even magical purposes, displayed by kings and queens and members of the nobility. Many such items were discovered in the tombs of Ur (c.2500) by Sir Leonard Woolley during excavations between 1922-1934 (see below). Craftsmen's guilds hid the 'secrets' of their skills derived from long experience and passed down as 'mysteries' from father to son, thus protecting their power and means of livelihood.

The presence of all these exotic items in Sumer consisting of valuable items for investment, implies a substantial trade after the fifth millennium BC. From long distances (perhaps by donkey or onager caravans), they brought from dealers in Afghanistan (Bactria, Sogdiana) nearly 2000 miles to the east, lapis lazuli and other semi-precious stones, listed above. They must have passed through the hands of a number of merchants with established trading stations *en route*. Thus, it would be very rare for a Sumerian trader to make a return journey of about 4000 miles to bring the precious lapis lazuli home. The wheel appeared from beyond the Caucasus. (c.3100). Wagons with four solid wheels replaced sledges which had been dragged over smoothed surfaces, and military chariots were in use early in the third millennium, as depicted on the Standard of Ur. The Sumerians also learned to use the wheel for pottery work.

From unearthed artefacts and inscriptions of unknown peoples of Babylonia, archaeologists and philologists gradually reconstructed the histories of ancient cities, built progressively as from around 4500. The Sumerian buildings were the first to be discovered. Some temples and palaces on the top of mounds, dominating them, concealed even earlier buildings.

At Uruk German archaeologists unearthed an occupation stratum of less than 40 feet thick, representing a very long period. Excavations by British archaeologists at Eridu revealed 14 temples one above the other. Its city walls had a perimeter of six miles. The remains of numerous cemeteries, temples and palaces stand witness to the increasing populations of important cities. The cemetery at Eridu, the secular capital of Sumer, contained more than a thousand graves.[2]

Uruk had a population of about 25,000. Canals with their sluices were from the very first indispensable. Roads had evolved by the middle of the third millennium as essential links of communication with the world outside the city walls.

These achievements, certainly well before 3000 BC, imply ready availability of the basic necessities of life: secure food supplies and an abundance of water, shelter for ordinary folk, palaces for kings and nobles, and temples for gods and priests, which altogether, represent the hierarchy of the social structure. The gods were honoured with impressive temples and regular seasonal festivals; and the king, as the father of his people, was feared and respected. He maintained a highly disciplined army for their protection against possible aggressors. They were exhorted to be good to their parents, their wives, their children, their neighbours, and to help those who were sick and feeble; to speak well of people; to practice kindness and compassion, sincerity, and a respect for the laws of the land. In return for such obedience and piety, the precepts set by the gods, a man, surrounded by his family, received protection in times of danger, comfort in distress, and honour, wealth, long life and happiness. Their religion and their arts and, above all, the impression they give of a peace-loving people puts them on a par with and often superior to other civilized communities that have come and gone during the long course of history, down to our own times.

Wealth in the form of large acres and the harnessed energies and talents of slaves, craftsmen, and astute civil servants, was accumulated by the mighty few, whose ancestral power would have originated in brute force, and a modicum of organising ability and leadership. They established great aristocratic dynasties. The very existence of the priest-king and the state depended on their support. These factors constitute an advanced social structure but they would fail and fall if the means were not available for recording the items of wealth, the manner of their acquisition and disposal and the day-to-day business transactions and other events, particularly the advertisement of the laws of the land. For these purposes, the invention of writing was the catalyst between primitive and civilized life. It is significant that the earliest writing coincides with the appearance of monumental architecture, especially temples,[3] where the priests developed increasingly sophisticated means of recording the quantity-fluctuations of the food stocks in their warehouses for distribution to the people.

WRITING: In late fourth millennium BC, over 5,000 years ago, writing emerged from Uruk (Erech). It promulgated to posterity the rise of Sumer as the first known literate society. We describe its wedge-shaped character as the 'cuneiform script', easy to reproduce with a sharp instrument, on brick tablets made with soft clay. Its significance cannot be overestimated; it represents man's greatest achievement since his discovery of fire, and how to make and use tools. Writing perpetuates the experience of past generations. It accelerated the development of Sumer. Its successors – Babylon, Assyria and others – adopted its cuneiform script.

Sumerian is the oldest known literary language of mankind, surpassing even Egyptian in age; the earliest known inscriptions come from the late fourth millennium, perhaps a century or two before the earliest Egyptian inscriptions, and the oldest now known literary texts date from about the

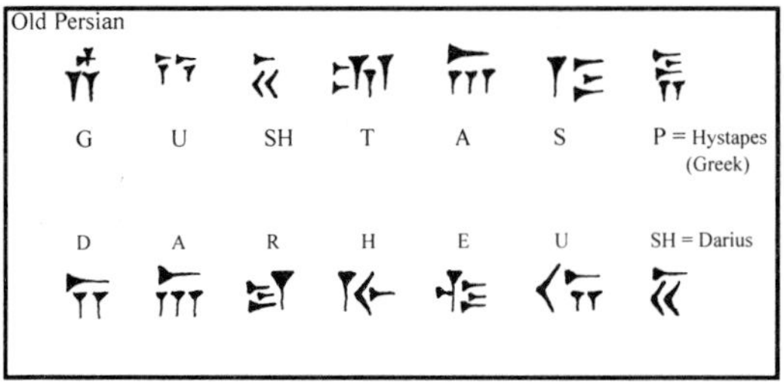

Figure 4. Old Persian script. After Leonard Cottrell, Reading the Past.

26th century BC Shuruppak, (Fara or Tell Farah) and Tell abu Salabikh. As the language of the first known high culture, it ultimately influenced the West far more than Egypt could. It became extinct as a spoken language, for all practical purposes, soon after the close of Ur Third Dynasty, at the end of the third millennium BC (2006 BC), but was intensively cultivated by scribes down into the second century BC, if not even later. [4]

Mesopotamian scribes bequeathed tablets of school textbooks and a wealth of translations of official correspondence and ancient literary texts, such as the epics of *The Creation* and *Gilgamesh* (c.2800), down to the second century BC, a literary tradition which was unbroken for 3000 years. This desire to transmit to their contemporaries and to posterity details of their way of life in a written form was in itself an important cultural trait of Mesopotamian civilization. By the seventh century BC there was a large number of private collectors of cuneiform texts, culminating in the great libraries of Assyria's King Ashurbanipal (668-624 BC). The cuneiform alphabet continued to be used even in the Hellenistic period, down to c. 190 BC. The ancient Sumerian and Akkadian texts were taught to foreign scribes, just as in Western Europe's Middle Ages, Latin and Greek became part of every scholar's training.

European scholars' attention was first drawn to cuneiform writing early in the seventeenth century by travellers in Persia. In 1760, Karsten Niebuhr, a German, established the validity of the reports. He not only returned from Persepolis with copies of some cuneiform inscriptions, but was also able to distinguish three different forms of the script, one of them appearing to be words with an alphabetical construction. It was assumed that the scripts were in the Old Persian language, for they were copied from carvings on the remains of the palaces of the Persian Great Kings, especially Darius the Great and Xerxes (fifth century BC).

Early in the first decade of the nineteenth century, a young German school-master, George Friedrich Grotefend, having noticed that ancient inscriptions of a king began with his name, title and antecedents, and knowing the source of Niebuhr's copies, had only to try the names of Xerxes son of Darius, son of Hystaspes. By guessing the Persian forms of these names, Grotefend succeeded in establishing the sounds of fourteen Old Persian characters, twelve of which later proved to be correct.

He presented a paper offering the methods of his findings to the Academy of Sciences in 1802, but they rejected it, because he was not an orientalist. It remained to be announced to the world in the appendix of a friend's book. Grotefend translated not only the three Persian names, but also part of the rest of the inscriptions, as follows:

> Darius, Great King, King of kings. King of the lands,
> son of Hystaspes, successor of the ruler of the world.

This remarkable beginning was carried on by scholars such as Lassen of Bonn (c.1845). At about the same time, a British army officer and diplomat in Persia, Henry Rawlinson (1810-1895), had noticed long inscriptions, carved high on the rock face of a cliff at Bisitun or Behistun, Kermanshah, Persia. He contrived to climb up to it and make a precise copy. As he recognised resemblances in the languages of the Persian inscriptions and that of the Old Persian or the Avesta and Sanskrit, their congruence had to be accepted.

Of the other two scripts at Bisitun, Akkadian was one and Elamite the other. The two main dialects of Akkadian were Babylonian and Assyrian, of which Babylonian was the most important. The methods used to decipher the Old Persian, starting with proper names and titles, were not always rewarding. The most fundamental contributions were made by Isidor Löwenstern (1845): that there were links between the ancient (Aryan) Akkadian and the modern Semitic (e.g. Arabic and Hebrew) languages; and the Rev. Edward Hincks (1850): that the different signs represented syllables. The first striking evidence of the power of writing which has come down to us is the great Sumerian Epic of *Gilgamesh*, written in the cuneiform script: it tells the story of the Great Flood. It has some credibility and much historical interest. It narrates the adventures of king Gilgamesh of Uruk (c.2800), whose beloved companion, Enkidu, dies. While in search of his friend, and the secret of eternal life, in the nether world, Gilgamesh meets Uta-napishtim, the Sumerian Noah, a member of the assembly of the gods, who tells him the story of the Great Flood.

He says that he was a citizen of Shurrupak (somewhat to the north-east of Eridu), between the two great rivers. The irrigated areas of that open, uncultivated steppe served as pasture land and was called, in Sumerian, 'Edin', a word from which the Biblical 'Eden' – the Garden of Eden – might well have been derived. It had a shrine of the god Tammuz, the son-lover of the goddess Bahu, manifestation of the most ancient (Palaeolithic) Great Earth Mother, who, in various guises, has come down to our own times, and many of us today worship and adore her, as did early men and women. They dwelt there, in the shade of the same sacred tree. They often appear on Akkadian sculptures. A cylinder seal now at the British Museum, the Seal of Temptation, shows the figures of a man and a woman seated on each side of a tree, with hands stretched towards it. Behind the woman, an upright snake is to be seen.

> The city of Shurrupak, [says Uta-Napishtim], grew old, and the people multiplied, and the world roared like a wild bull, our lord, Enlil, was angered by the clamour. He called a council of the gods, and said, 'we can no longer tolerate the uproar of mankind'. So, in secret, the gods decided to let loose the Deluge; but in a dream, my good lord Ea whispered their words to my house of reeds, for he and the council of gods had vowed secrecy: 'O man of Shurrupak pull down your house and build a boat. These are the measurements of the vessel that you shall build: Let the beam equal the length, and let the deck be covered like the vault of a cave; then take up into

the boat the seed of all living creatures. [5,6,7]

Uta-napishtim's story continues much as that in the Book of Genesis (written long after the Sumerian cuneiform version). That non-Biblical evidence was found by pure accident in 1872, when George Smith, a self-taught young man employed by the Department of Asiatic Antiquities at the British Museum, was cataloguing and repairing inscribed clay tablets, from the great library of King Ashurbanipal of Assyria (seventh century BC) which went back to the early part of the third millennium BC. Suddenly, in utter astonishment, he read:

> I looked about for coast lines in the sea:
> In each of fourteen regions.
> There emerged a region – a Mountain.
> On mount Nisir the ship came to rest.
> Mount Nisir held the ship fast,
> Allowing no motion.
> One day, and a second day, Mount Nisir held the ship fast
> Allowing no motion . . .
> When the seventh day arrived,
> I sent forth and set free a dove.
> The dove went forth, but came back;
> It could not find a resting place.
> I then sent forth a swallow,
> And she returned likewise.
> Next I sent forth a raven, and she flew away.
> She saw that the waters were shrinking,
> And gorged and croaked and waded,
> But did not come back.

It is said that George Smith, in his excitement, threw off his clothes and ran around as if he had taken leave of his senses. Eventually, on 3 December, 1872, he read a paper on the historical evidence of a Biblical Narrative, to the Society of Biblical Archaeology. On a grant of £1,000 given to him by the *Daily Telegraph* newspaper he went to Aleppo to dig for more evidence. He discovered over 3,000 inscribed tablets. Only three years later he had succeeded in piecing together a complete version of the Mesopotamian Flood story, when he died of dysentery in Aleppo (1876). Here then is proof of the incalculable value of writing, which the people of ancient Sumer invented, and an example of the extremely valuable documents which they and their successors have bequeathed to us.

> The Flood stories as told in the cuneiform scripts make it clear that the name given by the Sumerians to Noah was Ziusudra [Uta-napishtim in Gilgamesh], who reigned as king in the south Babylonian city of Shuruppak [modern Farah] probably at the end of the period known as Early Dynastic I (c.3000). We have every reason to believe that Ziusudra was indeed an historical figure, for archaeology has substantiated the existence of mythological Hero-Kings, such as Gilgamesh and others, who followed him in the most ancient columns of the Sumerian king-list. . . . [7]

TRADE and incidental exploration for markets and sources of supply continued on an ever increasing scale in the fourth millennium (early Bronze Age). The great rivers were the obvious highways between Sumer and Babylonia in the

Figure 5. A cylinder seal from Sumer. Courtesy, Trustees of the British Museum.

south, and Anatolia in the north. Anatolia was rich in minerals of almost every description mainly in the east, while in the centre, the Amanus mountain regions offered much needed timber. In earliest times (before the appearance and establishment of Hittite and Hurrian cities), there would have been a demand in the north for the manufactures of the more advanced craftsmen in Mesopotamia, whence traders could have loaded their donkey or onager caravans with leather (shields and helmets of Mesopotamian soldiery (c.2300) were made of leather), as well as manufactured goods, such as textiles in linen and wool, and embroidery; perhaps also earthenware, expertly fashioned out of the abundant clay in the south, for domestic use or ornamental purposes. Assuming much more advanced societies in the south than in the north, there would have been a demand in the north for metalworkers bronze tools and weapons, copper vessels, carpenters utensils, precious or semi-precious stones for personal adornment, prestige or investment, such as jewellery fashioned from lapis lazuli, obsidian, diorite, steactite, cowrie shells. The bulkier items might be hauled up river in small boats.

These were bartered for much needed timber. The heavy tree trunks could be floated down river, much as they are today in Canada and elsewhere. The problem of carrying heavy building stones and metal ores, such as copper (in abundance in the border region between Anatolia and northern Syria) and the obsidian volcanic rocks from both the Ararat and Amanus regions, was solved by the use of small boats or rafts buoyed by inflated skins, and floated down the Euphrates or Tigris, for sale in the southern cities most of which were situated very near the rivers.

> The circular boats which came down the river to Babylon are made of willow frames and covered with skins. They are then entirely filled with straw, their cargo is put on board and they are then suffered to float down stream . . . The boats are of various sizes, the biggest reach as high as 5000 talents' burthen. Each vessel has a live ass on board; those of larger size have more than one. When they reach Babylon where the cargo, including the straw and frames, is sold, they load their asses with skins and set off on their way back to Armenia, where they build fresh boats for the next voyage. Herodotus (I.194)

Timber and metal ores and stones were also imported from the Zagros areas in the east. Amber came from Scandinavia, via the Adriatic sea, quite early in the period.

Those early merchants hauled their small boats against the current of the river (or led their caravans along the river valley) to northern Syria where a brief portage to the Orontes gave access to the Port of Poseideïon (al Mina), and a short sea crossing to Cyprus and its wealth of copper, as well as to the long Mediterranean littoral, and southward, to the great ports, such as Ugarit and Byblos.

The Sumerians also ventured out in ships made of their native reeds into the unknown, dark Indian Ocean. They turned westwards along the coast of Arabia, and so into the Red Sea (as demonstrated in recent years by Thor Heyerdahl), which led them to one of the tributaries of the Nile, perhaps today's Wadi Hammamat, and so to Egypt (see chapter 5). They also learnt the eastward sea-route from the Gulf to northern India where, for some 2,000 years, flourished the highly advanced Indus or Harappan civilization of Harappa and Mohenjo-Daro in the Punjab region, an area about the size of France. That civilization died before the end of the second millennium BC:

> It is legitimate to affirm that the *idea* of civilization came to the land of the
> Indus from the land of the Twin Rivers.[8]

It was first cited by the Greek geographer Strabo (XV.i.19). Its geometrical town planning system, with broad streets, was enhanced by a sophisticated drainage system. A bathroom, floored with finely joined bricks, has an earthenware pipe encased in brickwork which carried the waste to a courtyard and street drain. Another earthenware pipe, built vertically into one of the walls, carried drainage from the roof. Like others, that civilization, too, must have had an organised agricultural system and trading traditions. The Sumerians traded with an area or place they called 'Meluhha', in the Harappan region, whence they probably brought home spices, among other exotic items described by Sir Mortimer Wheeler.

Jacquetta Hawkes[9] writes:

> That part of the Kulli people who lived in the Makran had learnt to make
> one fine product . . . . This was a substance, probably some scented unguent,
> that they put up in well finished stone jars. This product . . . was in such
> demand that the luxury trade carried it as far as Syria. . . . Considerable
> numbers of these have been found in Mespoptamia, including one in the
> grave of Queen Shub-ad in the famous cemetery of Ur.

In the absence of money, corn was a universally acceptable means of exchange. It could be transported in convenient quantities, it was divisible into lots of very small value, it did not putrefy easily and it could be stored in large jars for long periods. The merchants of those early city states soon understood the convenience of credit transactions, and by 2000, they had grasped the complications of payment by bills of exchange and dealing in 'futures', when an astute dealer might buy crops before the season, in anticipation of probable scarce supply and relative high demand, and commanding a much higher price than at the time of purchase.

RELIGION: The temples, the 'Houses of the Gods', stand witness to the universal principle that religion is a great cohesive factor in the corporate life of a people. The colossal temples must have been built somewhat in the same spirit of fear and love of god as were the great cathedrals of the European Middle Ages – with

Figure 6. Spouted limestone offering pitcher from Uruk (c. 2800 BC). Ht 20.3 cm, dia. 11.5 cm. Artistic technique is so far advanced, even as early as this as to depict such a complicated subject as the struggle of a lion with a bull in miniature. Iraq Museum, Baghad.

unremitting labour and dedication, by successive generations of the same craftsmen families. Nippur was the religious centre and home of the god Enlil. Eridu was the temporal capital.

The Sumerians, like their successors, had many gods. But one supreme god for each city, for whom they toiled, whose wars they fought, whose priests they revered and whom they supplied with 'Houses of God'. They worked for them, paid them tribute, supplied them with virgins (ostensibly for the god) who became temple prostitutes – a tradition which continued for many centuries almost until the Christian era. All the lesser city-gods were killed off in battle together with their priest-king. At the end, there remained the God of gods – An, King of Heaven, Enki, Lord of the Earth (and their wives and children) and later among the most powerful, the Babylonian God of gods, Marduk.

Largely like the city states of Classical Greece and Medieval Italy, those of Sumer were also independent states. Each had its own ruler and its own chief god with his subordinate 'saints', who represented one or other aspect of the universe and life on earth. The ruler or king was often also the high priest, hence the priest-king. Defeat in war resulted in the loss of the chief god's effigy, which was carried away in triumph by the conqueror, to be placed in an inferior position within the hierarchy of his own gods. By implication, the spiritual power of the defeated king would also vanish, if indeed he had not himself been made prisoner or killed in battle. That would not be the end of the matter, however, for the conqueror would add the conquered city to his possessions. Later on, by virtue of additional conquests, he became 'Great King' and finally 'King of Kings'.

Thus, government of the ancient oriental kingdoms was invariably theocratic; the priest-king was the supreme autocrat, the strength of Sumerian society. He

Figure 7. Cylinder seal of red and white jasper and its modern impression, with heroes fighting lions and a cuneiform inscription. Akkadian, probably from southern Iraq, about 2250 BC. Ht. 3.6 cm. Courtesy, Trustees of British Museum.

also personified the vigour of a highly disciplined army. Out of a total area of about 1,800 square miles representing, the city-state of Lagash, approximately 670 square miles of it was an inalienable part of the temple and could not change ownership. The total population of the city would have been some 30,000 to 35,000.[10] One part of the estate, 'the land of the Lord', was set aside for the sustenance of the priests and other inmates of the temple itself. Those who worked on it – the farmers – were allotted (not given) the 'food land', small parcels of land for their own subsistence, and the remainder, the 'plough land' was let out to tenants for about one-seventh of the produce. Surpluses were stored in the temple warehouse against unforeseen disasters, or for export, against barter.[12]

The texts mention only freemen and slaves within the social structure. The slaves, as ever, were at the bottom of the system. Not very numerous, they were recruited from prisoners of war or kidnapped, usually from abroad. The peasants and servants of the temple or the palace were maintained by the priests and the king respectively and did not possess any land. The freemen consisted of a large group of landowners, and the remainder of the population comprised all kinds of farmers, artisans, merchants, the aristocracy and the royal family. These were the people within the city state, a very large acreage surrounding the city itself, all of which was ruled by the king.[11]

The individual was well integrated into the community and so acted with a corporate mind and will to survive invasions and universal catastrophes such as floods, droughts, encroachment of the sea, storms and earthquakes, always, of course, under the benevolent auspices of celestial intervention. The concept of the gods of that most ancient world was only that of superhuman beings and they were, in that sense, within the ethos of the community and an essential part of it.

This should not be difficult for us to understand, even though 5000 years separate us from Sumer, for many of us clutch the metaphorical hand of a powerful Being we call God or Jesus, Allah or Mohammed, Jehovah or Moses. Perhaps our concept of God and his powers might not be so specific as those of our ancestors. For we become ever more sophisticated as we unravel (so we think) the puzzles of the nature of the universe and the physical life-giving bodies in it – the sun, the moon and the planets of our own tiny area of the cosmos. But in the last analysis, as our individual energies wane at an increasing pace from birth to old age, as disasters with which we cannot cope or even comprehend, overtake us, we do turn for support to Something unseen – until we understand the nature of our troubles. That wise astronomer, philosopher and king of Samarkand, Ulugh Beg (c.AD 1430), pointed out that where science begins

religion ends. But he failed to say that if man ever understood all Knowledge, than he would surely cease to be man, and theological discussions would be irrelevancies.

Belief in an afterlife of some kind, seems to be universal. The grave of a youth of the Old Stone Age (Neanderthal), who had been laid down with his head upon his right forearm to rest upon a pillow of stones, was uncovered in modern times. The Sumerian idea of life hereafter was hopelessness – ghosts of the dead generally had a miserable time. Yet this contradicts the idea of opulence and pleasure in the hereafter, implied by the findings in the royal graves at Ur (and elsewhere), where kings were buried with their wives, servants, jewellery and chattels.

Philosophers such as Plato and Spinoza, and beliefs such as Hinduism, reject the continuation of the individual's identity after death, but believe in the all-pervasiveness of a universal Spirit which manifests itself in multifarious organisms and organisations.

These are themselves microcosms of an unimaginably immense Mother-Father Macrocosmos. That idea seems to be an unconscious and endemic factor in human nature at all stages of human development. There has always been a supreme, powerful Mother Goddess to be worshipped and adored. Yet, in human society, the man is usually supreme and woman is supposed to take a secondary part in important matters. This situation has been prevalent in Judeo-Christian-Islamic mores. Among the Sumerians, the celestial powers were male, their wives were terrestrial females. However, they did not blame women for all the ills of this world. Among the celestial powers Tiamat, the fierce old 'Great Mother' of Sumerian folk, prevailed.

Human attitudes in this and other aspects of life are reflected in those of their gods. This is illustrated by the images of the gods fashioned by man. Just as there were powerful and weak men, rich and poor men, good and evil men, so there were corresponding gods: chief gods and lesser gods, good gods and evil gods, large and well endowed temples, and small, humble ones. From the beginning of the Bronze Age (c.3000), these factors seem to have been recognised. Power rested with the wily Priest-king who knew how his subjects could best be kept in hand by fear, ritual, holy days and sacrifices. He had to be careful, if he was thoughtful as well as wily, for man reflects the image of his god, and vice-versa. A cruel and vicious god (represented by his priest) produces his kind of worshippers; a good god produces good people, but their priest-king can harness the good for evil purposes. Christianity has basically a good God but the purveyors of that religion have often been corrupt as well as ignorant, with horrifying results.

The chief Sumerian gods appear to have been good gods, upholding Justice and Truth. But in real life, there were always evil persons, landlords who oppressed their poor tenants, creditors who charged ruinous interest rates, unjust and cruel heads of families, and so forth. Hence, Good and Evil had to exist together, as they did then and they do today. For we would not understand the measure of Good without a knowledge of Evil. Thus Satan has a function.

All this should illustrate how little are the fundamental differences between the ancient social framework and that of our own. Theirs was a truly theocratic city-state but ours, a development from the king who was wholly subservient to the church, during the Middle Ages, to the representative of God on earth, the Pope; developing into a royal personage who is either a despot with divine powers or, beyond such a monarch, more reasonably to one who is 'Defender of the Faith'. Therefore, protocol requires that the Priest-king precedes the High Priest, who is followed by the secular 'prime minister', under whatsoever title he might be described. The power of the Church and Religion, for good or ill, is fully recognised by the modern state, whether or not the 'House of God' (church, mosque, synagogue, temple) is within the constitution of the state (as in England). THE LAWS. This suggestion is supported by the laws of the Sumerian city-states whose kings seem to have had a sense of justice, without which, indeed, the highly disciplined life of a civilized state would not be conceivable. Urukagina of Lagash (c.2351-2342), a righteous king, whose maxim was to restrain the rapacious tax collector, to cut down the power of the temple priests and the lay officials of the palace, and to abolish the various extortionate fees and dues to which the vizier as well as the governor, or the king himself, had a right. He put down thieves, robbers and noble rogues and during the whole period of his reign there was peace and stability in his kingdom. Among other just laws, there were those respecting divorce and the protection of widows and orphans against the 'strong man'.

Urukagina was attacked and defeated by Lugal-zagesi (c. 2340-2316), the ensi (governor) of Umma, a neighbouring city, who proclaimed himself to be its king. He made the city of Erech (Uruk, Warka), his capital, whence he dominated the whole (that is, all the city-states) of Sumer, including the important city of Kish, near Babylon. Then he overran Syria and reached the Mediterranean. His empire extended 'from the sea of the rising sun to the sea of the setting of the sun' and the god Enlil 'made straight my path from the Lower Sea, unto the Upper Sea' (from the Persian Gulf to the Mediterranean). Thus was the intellectual king Urukagina defeated, by the warrior Lugal-zagesi, who unwittingly laid the foundations of the dominion over Syria by the Semitic kings of Akkad, who were soon to appear.[12]

Two-hundred years later, Ur-Nammu (c.2113 BC), the founder of the third dynasty of Ur, is reputed to have conformed to the just laws of the sun-god, Utu (Shamash), so that 'the orphan and the widow were not delivered up to the rich and mighty, and the man of one mina did not overbear the man of one shekel'. The laws of Nammu anticipated some of the basic principles of modern justice. He instituted a scale of fines, in accordance with the seriousness of misdeeds, be they intentional or accidental: if a man cuts off another 'man's foot', by accident or design, he shall be fined ten shekels of silver. But that amount seems to have been a kind of standard which could be decreased if the victim was a slave or increased if the victim was a nobleman, which, to us, would appear to be unjust, although the punishment takes the form of a forfeit rather than the Semitic *lex talionis*: an eye for an eye, a tooth for a tooth.[13]

A king of Larsa, is called 'the shepherd of justice'. By the time the dynasty of Larsa fell (the last Sumerian dynasty (2025-1762)), the Sumerians had given . first to their northern Semitic neighbours and somewhat later to wild Semitic Chaldean and Aramean conquerors, all the requirements of a true civilization: an alphabet, humane laws, economic stability, religious conformity (necessary for the discipline of ignorant peasants and the fearful superstitions of their betters which was and still is in many places, the way of life in Christian Europe), fully developed arts and crafts and architecture which sometimes also demanded engineering skills (implying an advanced scientific knowledge) which were at that time, long before the Ionians, mainly empirical. The examples of ethical concepts upon which the foundations of Sumerian civilization rested, are in contrast to the vengeful and cruel laws of the early Semites, based upon the *lex talionis*, which on the larger scene of history leads to barbarity and merciless war. Some of the kings of the third dynasty of Ur, e.g. Ur-Nammu, Shulgi, added lustre to the fading light of venerable Sumer which had bequeathed to posterity the invaluable gift of literacy. Ur fell to Amorite invasions from the western desert after prolonged resistance of over twenty years, when it was also invaded by Elam.

One of the most moving of Sumerian poems records the catastrophe:
Dead men, not potsherds,/Covered the approaches,/The walls were gaping,/ the high gates, the roads were piled with dead./In the side streets, where feasting crowds would gather,/Scattered they lay,/In all the streets and roadways bodies lay. In open fields that used to fill with dancers, they lay in heaps./The country's blood now filled its holes,/like metal in a mould;/Bodies dissolved – like fat in the sun. [14]

ARTS AND CRAFTS: In those early times, there was no 'art for art's sake'. Art was usually functional. Beauty in art was incidental. Yet, a strong sense of symmetry and what is pleasing to the eye was instinctively achieved. Indeed, in their architecture the Sumerians prove their awareness of the importance of its aesthetic aspects. They built certain features of their temples, for example, slightly out of alignment in order to correct optical illusions (called *entasis*). Art was not intended for the representation of everyday life; it depicted and perpetuated the image of power – gods, priests, kings, with their great, bulging eyes and naked bodies. And goddesses, with woman's naturally half-secret as well as naturally fully exposed and often beautiful vehicles of creation and sustenance of life. Their worshippers are also depicted, some cringing in the act of veneration, some smiling complacently. These could be either figurines in the round, or single figures painted on monuments and vases, or engraved on the walls and columns

Figure 9. Alabaster vase with figures and decoration in relief. 105cm high (c.3200 BC). From Uruk, Iraq Museum, Baghdad.

of temples, palaces, and public buildings.

The lay world was served not by 'artists' but by craftsmen and artisans – potters, stonemasons, carvers in wood, goldsmiths, silversmiths, bronzesmiths. From as early as the fourth millennium, there is evidence of extremely sensitive and beautiful artistic products. An outstanding example is the deservedly famous alabaster vase from Uruk (c.3200). Elegantly conceived, it stands 1.05 m. high and bears upon its surface reliefs of naked men carrying dishes containing offerings of the produce of the land, to the goddess of fertility. That urn, now exhibited at the Iraq Museum, Baghdad, is no amateur's work; a king could have been its proud possessor.

It is an outstanding example of the principle that works of art are preserved from one generation to the next, for centuries or millennia, for two reasons (a) because of their intrinsic beauty, which is appreciated by all comers, through successive generations; (b) just because of their historical interest, indicating perhaps, a stage in the evolution of the particular means of artistic expression, be it in plastic or graphic form. It might also represent a

Figure 10. 'The Standard of Ur', detail showing the Sumerian army going into battle. Courtesy, Trustees of the British Museum.

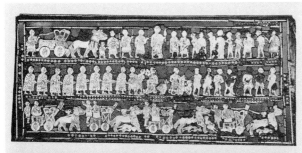

Figure 11. 'The Standard of Ur'. Shell, red limestone and lapis lazuli inlaid into a bitumen base. Rectangular object originally of wood decorated with stone and shell mosaic. Use unknown, ht 20.3 cm. (c. 2500 BC.) From the royal grave at Ur, Babylonia. Courtesy, Trustees of the British Museum

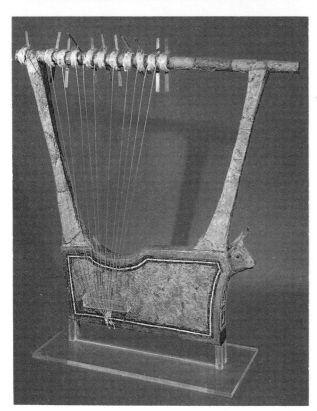

Figure 12. Silver lyre with inlaid front, from 'The Great Death Pit' at Ur, c. 2500 BC. Courtesy, Trustees of the British Museum.

parallelism with other aspects of the total culture of the people which is expressed by the creative works of its artist-craftsmen. Thus, every generation has admired the beautiful products of the artists of Classical Greece, because of their undoubted, intrinsic beauty. On the other hand, we gaze on and study the stiff and sometimes ugly products of some primitive societies

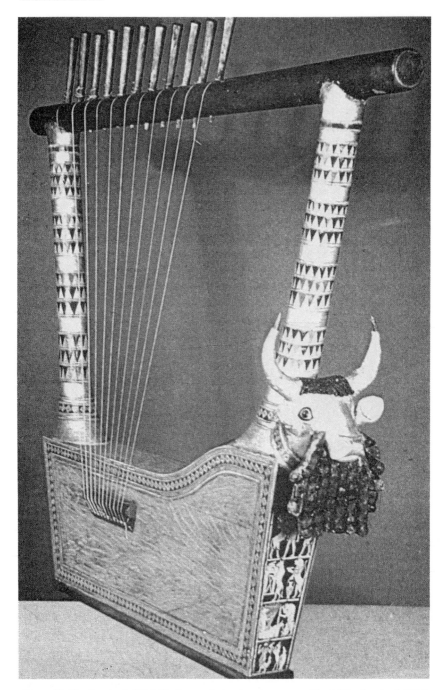

Figure 13. 'The Standard of Ur'. The lyre as depicted on the reverse side of 'The Standard of Ur'. Courtesy, Trustees of the British Museum.

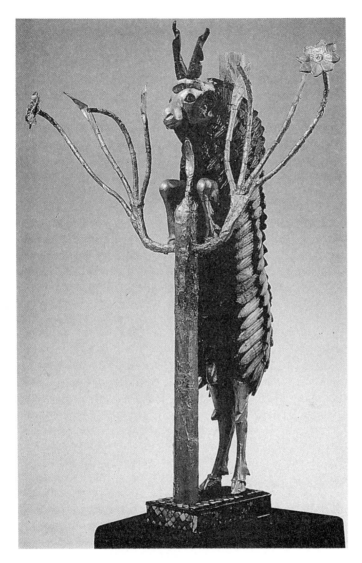

Figure 14. Symbolic figure of a goat about to nibble at a tree. Made of shell, lapis lazuli and gold; sometimes associated with the Biblical 'Ram caught in a thicket'. Sumerian, c. 2500 BC, Ur, ht 45.7 cm. Courtesy, Trustees of the British Museum.

only because they are of historical or social interest. In this category modern examples abound.

The royal cemetery at Ur (c.2500 BC), excavated by Sir Leonard Woolley in 1922-34, was rich with beautiful artefacts. The objects of gold, silver, and precious stones which were brought out of the 1,850 graves, are original in conception beautiful in appearance and unique in the history of civilization. They stand witness to a high standard of art which is comparable to the artistic achievements of any other period in history.

One of the areas excavated was the cemetery where 1840 graves of the 3rd

Figure 15. Gold head of a Bull. Ornament on the sounding box of a lyre from the 'Royal Cemetery of Ur', c. 2500 BC. Courtesy, Trustees of the British Museum.

millennium BC were found. Seventeen of these were particularly rich, and form what Woolley called 'The Royal Cemetery'. In most of these rich graves there was more than one skeleton, and in one ('The Great Death Pit') 74 bodies were found lying in rows. Various theories have been put forward to explain the slaughter, the most common being that servants were killed in order to accompany their master in the afterlife.

Inscriptions found in two graves identify the owners: one was A-kalan-du, king of Ur (Grave 1050) and the other was Queen Pu-abi (Grave 800). . . .

These Sumerian royal graves can now be dated to the latter part of the Early Dynastic Period, about 2500 BC.[15]

Lady Woolley (who had accompanied her husband) modelled a female head and decorated it with the exotic, unique jewellery of Queen Pu-abi. It is now exhibited at the British Museum, London, together with the rest of the artefacts of the royal graves of Ur. From grave 1237 came a beautifully conceived model of a goat, standing upright on its hind legs, apparently entangled in the branches of a tree. Its wooden core is covered by gold and silver sheets, it has shell-covered horns, its beard and neck are of lapis lazuli. It is reminiscent of the Biblical 'Ram caught in a thicket' (Gen.XXII.13).

Grave 779 produced, among other interesting articles, the celebrated 'Standard of Ur'. 'The purpose of this 'standard' is not known.' (It might be the sounding-box of a musical instrument). It is 'a double-sided panel on which tiny figures in shell or mother-of-pearl are inlaid in bitumen against a mosaic of lapis lazuli.'16 It shows a harp, topped by a decorative bull's head. An almost precise model of that harp was discovered in one of the royal graves. The outstanding feature of the instrument, the bull's head, has a wooden core which is covered with gold sheets. These magnificent items from Ur are exhibited at the British Museum.

Like most aspects of Life, the rationale of which is unknown to mankind, the problems of birth and death can be discussed, argued and philosophised *ad infinitum*. The interested reader is referred for more detailed ideas and discussion, elsewhere, including some of the sources suggested below.

Notes

1. Wheeler Mortimer, *The Indus Civilization*, Cambridge University Press, 1968, p. 35.
2. Burney Charles, *From Village to Empire*, Phaidon, Oxford, 1977.
3. Rowton M.B., 'Ancient Western Asia', CAH I¹, pp. 226-7.
4. Albright W.F., and Lambdin T.O., 'The Evidence of Language', CAH I¹ ,p. 145.
5. Sandsars N.K., *The Epic of Gilgamesh*, Penguin, London, 1972.
6. Mallowan Max L., The Development of Cities from Al-'Ubaid to the end of Uruk, CAH I¹, p. 354.
7. Solberger Edmond, *The Flood*, British Museum Publications, 1977.
8 Wheeler Mortimer, *The Indus Civilization*, Cambridge University Press, 1971, pp. 25, 49, 81, 115, 129.
9. Hawkes Jaquetta, *The First Civilizations*, Hutchinsons, 1973, pp. 82, 83.
10. Frankfort H., *Town Planning Review 21*, 1950; I.M. Diakonoff, *Journal of Ancient History*, Moscow, 1950-2, quoted by George Roux, *Iraq*, London 1950.
11. Diakonoff I.M., *Sales of Land in Pre-sargonic Sumer*, Moscow, 1954; quoted by George Roux, op.cit.
12. Rowton M.B., 'Ancient Western Asia', *CAH I¹*, pp. 219-220.
13. Oates Joan , *Babylon*, Thames & Hudson, London, 1979, p. 74-6.
14. *ibid.* p. 52.
15. Mitchell T.C., *Sumerian Art Illustrated by Objects from Ur and Al-'Ubaid*, British Museum Publications, 1979.
16. Seton Lloyd, *The Art of the Ancient Near East*, Thames & Hudson, London, 1965, pp. 84-85.

Authors Note – The Ayran group of languages from remote, prehistoric times, originated in northern India and Afghanistan (Bactria, Sogdiana). It is usually (misleadingly) called *Indo-European* because most European languages stem from it. When referring to any one of that group of languages I have used either Indo-European, Indo-Ayran of Ayran to describe them.

Chapter 3
Babylon

It is often difficult to identify by name the various groups of peoples – nomadic tribes, barbaric invaders – who periodically burst out from the Arabian desert (or from the steppes of Central Asia). These peoples swarmed upon the settled communities along the great rivers, appropriated their possessions, killed their owners and made themselves masters of their cities.

Hordes of such invaders emerged from Arabia and struck the Palestine and Syrian coastlines, where they established themselves. They are generally identified as 'Amurru' (Biblical Amorites), Habiru ('homeless outlaws'), Hebrews and other Amorites, who settled as near the powerful Sumerian cities as they dared (c.2600). All these nomads and raiders from Arabia were Semitic peoples or Semites who spoke a group of related languages.

> The Sumerians themselves were conscious that to the west of their land . . .
> they had neighbours whose way of life was different from their own, uncouth
> nomads who lived in tents, ate meat uncooked, dug for truffles in the desert,
> and neglected to bury their dead. Though they regarded these westerners
> with fear and distaste, they permitted individual tribesmen to settle amongst
> them, and the names of these Amorites, together with the deities with which
> they were associated, Dagan, Hadad and Yerakh the moon god, make it clear
> they were of west Semitic speech.[1]

Not long after that expression of Sumerian toleration, the newcomers attacked and captured some of the cities, killed their rulers and made themselves the masters. A rough but intelligent people, ultimately, under their king Sargon I of Akkad (2335-2280), they created a confederation of city-states and eventually the first of the great Semitic Empires, centred in Akkad, Kish and finally in Babylon. The upper half of that empire was called Akkad, the lower half Sumer, and the whole of it, Babylonia. Sargon's capitals, Kish and Akkad, are very close to Babylon on the Euphrates, roughly opposite modern Baghdad on the Tigris, where the gap between the two rivers is narrowest and of great strategic importance, both from political and commercial points of view. Legend has it that, as a baby, Sargon was discovered in a bitumen-lined basket, among reeds (which echoes the story of the Biblical Moses, (Exodus I)). Once he had united the whole of Babylonia Sargon could turn his attention to the conquest of the sophisticated cities in the west which were already within the Akkadian sphere

Figure 16. Bronze head from Nineveh. Probably portrait of King Sargon of Akkad c. 2300 BC, ht 30 cm. The sculpture expresses pride and nobility hitherto unattained in art. Iraq Museum, Bagdad.

of influence through mutual commercial interests. Also, access to the 'Upper Sea' (the Mediterranean) was an economic necessity. His empire included the powerful kingdoms of Ebla and Mari astride the trade routes into Syria, as well as those leading to the mineral rich Amanus and Taurus Mountains. According to some evidence, he even had intercourse with Egypt, Crete, Cyprus and almost certainly with some western parts of Anatolia, as well as eastwards with Elam and India – an empire of unprecedented extent.

Here, special reference must be made to the great-city state of Ebla (Tell Mardikh), south of Aleppo, which was discovered in 1964. An inscription on the torso of a statue in basalt, identified the city of Ebla. In 1973 an enormous palace dating to c. 2400 came to light, with a huge audience chamber, columned porches and a royal platform. The massive building was decorated by rich ornamentation, such as fine carvings in ivory and wood and a great staircase embellished with inlaid shells. It showed Ebla as a wealthy kingdom occupying an extensive territory, probably ruled by a powerful king. Excavations in 1978 were continued by Italian archaeologists. About 15,000 Sumerian tablets were discovered consisting of international treaties, legal and political documents, records of tributes received from vassal states, commercial documents and many literary and religious texts. Among the most important finds, were the earliest known dictionaries, from Sumerian to Semitic and vice versa, as well as much teaching material.

Such an empire, implies an ability to create a new hierarchy of astute governors and civil servants, and to learn and practice new forms of international diplomacy. Sargon's and his successors' acceptance of the Sumerian institutions such as the laws, the arts, the sciences as well as the gods is illustrated by the celebration of Akkadian victories in the temple of Enlil at Nippur, in accordance with Sumerian custom. The worship of the Sumerian gods was promoted throughout Babylonia and the colonies, thus giving cohesion to an empire composed of peoples with different social and political persuasions. Such an empire implies the marriage of the military might of Akkad with the important intellectual and spiritual traditions of Sumer. The diplomatic, commercial and daily language of the ordinary people of Sumer-Akkad, the *lingua franca*, was Akkadian, a Semitic language, while scholars and priests used the language of ancient Sumer. So in medieval Europe, Latin was for scholars and the Church, while various dialects became the everyday languages of Europe.

Sargon died after a reign of 55 years (2279). He was succeeded by his two sons, Rimush, who was assassinated only eight years after his accession (2278-70), and Manishtushu (2270-2255). The title of 'Great King' has been bestowed upon Manishtushu because he was able to continue the tight control exercised by his father over subject states. He is remembered particularly for having suppressed revolts of powerful and feuding desert sheiks and their tribes, over ownership of wells and partition of grazing lands.

Naram-Sin (2255-2218), son of the short-lived Rimush, and grandson of Sargon, called himself 'King of the Four Quarters of the World'. Following Manishtushu's precedent, troops made periodic sorties to subdue recalcitrant peoples or to seize new lands; they escorted caravans to Mediterranean ports across tribute-paying territories. Naram-Sin consolidated his grandfather's authority in northern Mesopotamia, adding new temples to those built by his father, Rimush, and using religion as a powerful binding force of his empire. He destroyed Ebla and built a palace and blockhouse at Brak, strategically situated between Nineveh and Mari, to serve as an important base for his military operations in northern Syria and Anatolia.

His conquests and deeds of valour and his claim to be a god, are sculpted in writing and art form, on the famous victory sandstone stele. It shows him trampling over the bodies of the enemy, while marching up a mountainside to its summit, marked by the star of the sun-god Utu or Shamash. On the mountain-top, another inscription, carved by the king of Elam, 1000 years later (c.1158), tells how he carried off the stele in triumph from Sippar (north of Babylon) to his own capital, Susa, which had once been an Akkadian colony. The stele, 2 metres high, is now exhibited at the Louvre, Paris.

Thus, artistic excellence in this, the third millennium, was not confined to Sumer, where the impressive artefacts, already described, were found in the royal cemetery at Ur. Naram-Sin's victory stele is but one example of outstanding artistry. There is also the wonderful life-size, bronze head from Nineveh, which might be a portrait of this king or one of his predecessors. In more recent times, the marvellous, lower portion of a naked body, hollow-cast in copper, found in northern Iraq, bears a dedicatory inscription to Naram-Sin, which establishes its undoubted Akkadian origin.

The disadvantage to ordinary people of being part of a great empire, was that they were ruled by a despot from a distant capital, who controlled immense areas. Previously, the power of the ruler of a city-state was limited to that city, and no further. Power regenerates itself indefinitely, if it is not curbed. Conquerors are notorious personifications of its abuse. Thus, Naram-Sin deified himself, 'The god Naram-Sin, the mighty god of Akkad.'

In Sumer all landed property had been administered by the priests. It had

Figure 17. The celebrated stele of Naram-Sin, King of Akkad, c. 2255-2218 BC. Red sandstone, ht 200 cm. The king stands high up a mountain path, while his victorious soldiers ascend along the paths below, trampling upon the enemy. This much valued stele was carried off by the Elamites as part of the spoils of war (c. 1155BC). Courtesy, Louvre, Paris.

belonged to the local god. But the private citizen had possessed his house, furniture and slaves. It had been a theocratic community. The newcomers, the Semites, developed capitalism. They, therefore, destroyed the theocentric state – though not by any means religion itself, which was, indeed, the cornerstone of political power.

According to Sumerian tradition of religious communism, all real estate, such as land, belonged to God, whose agent was the priest-king or the temple. It could not be bought or sold. That Sumerian tradition changed to the Babylonian-Semitic concept that while admittedly it belonged ultimately to God, everything, including land, could be bought, sold and administered by anyone on His behalf. That concept was reinforced by making the King the authority on whom rested one's welfare. It was the foundation of the hierarchical pyramid consisting of state functionaries, landowners and farmers, and the purveyors of all kinds of arts, crafts and other services, all depending upon the king. The monarch took precedence over the High Priest and often the king himself was also high priest, and even God-king. *L'Etat, c'est moi*, as the king of France declared even 3000 years later.

Those nearest to the throne, the secular and spiritual aristocracies, were of course the greatest beneficiaries of that organisation; they had to be generously patronised by the monarch, since his own power and the stability of the state depended upon their loyal support. Within such an organisation religion became the monopoly of the god-king and the ruling class. Ordinary people would look to their all-powerful king for justice and help – they would pray to him. Of course

Figure 18. This beautiful model of a nude girdled figure from northern Iraq is hollow cast in copper. It weighs 157 kg, diameter of the base is 65cm. In the dedicatory inscription Naram-Sin describes himself as 'King of the four quarters of the world'. Iraq Museum. Bagdad.

diplomacy dictated that the king should assuage priestly jealousies and ensure their allegiance by his generosity: grants of land, gold, women (under the guise of the sacrifice of their virginity to their local gods in the temples), and many privileges and many gifts were offered in the form of endowments to their temples and their gods, their high priests and the temple hierarchy.

The power of religion has been perpetuated down to our own day. In peacetime the gods are placated by ritualistic prayer, by sacrifice and the adoration of symbols which represent them. In time of war, particularly in or near the homeland, religion plays an enormously important rôle. An impressive example of this last situation in our own times, is provided by the atheistic Stalin's Russian state, which, during the German invasion in the Second World War, opened up its churches to the secretly devout people, to give them the spiritual support, the will, with which to continue the defence of their country.

Thus, while in Sumer religion appears to reflect a purely spiritual concept, in Akkadian-Babylonian theology the function of religion from the rulers' point of view, was sociopolitical rather than purely spiritual. It is a difference as between a monk's or ascetic's single-minded piety, and that of the established church which has sociopolitical interests, indeed, responsibilities. In modern times, too, the clergy have sometimes dramatically intervened for the people against the state when, in their opinion, it has abused its power.

After Naram-Sin (2218), the last of the great Akkadian kings, there was revolution and turmoil, a time of anarchy, described by contemporary scribes as 'Who was king? Who was not king?'

A Gutian dynasty [a wild people from the direction of the Zagros mountains] is recorded which survived perhaps a hundred years (c.2220-2120) although the extent of its authority remains in doubt. It would appear that Gutian domination extended at least briefly as far south as Umma, and perhaps even to Ur, but independent dynasties are attested both at Uruk and at Lagash during this period. Very little material evidence of Gutian rule survives; it is interesting to note, however, that like all other invaders of Mesopotamia they appear to have taken on the colour of their surroundings, even observing the local cults.[2]

Interminable wars between city-states all over Mesopotamia, and the intervention

Figure 19. Basalt pillar inscribed with the laws of King Hammurabi of Babylon (c. 1770 BC), ht 2.25m, showing the seated king and his scribe at the top of the pillar. Found in Susa where it had been taken as plunder from Babylon by the Elamites (12th century BC). Courtesy, Louvre, Paris.

of the Gutians, eventually resulted in the demise of the Akkadian dynasty and the appearance of Babylonian kings (c. 1895).

In this brief outline of the history of the ancient Near East the minor events and minor rulers must be ignored. Reference has already been made to the Sumerian city of Ur. It demonstrated a resurgence of Sumerian power and culture (the Third Dynasty of Ur 2112-2004). We bestride 200 years of turmoil, submission to Ur, and change: from Naram-Sin of Akkad, who died in 2218, to Hammurabi (1792-1750), the sixth king of the Amorite First Dynasty of Babylon, which had been founded 100 years earlier (c. 1895).

The world had become a humming, busy place, peopled by noblemen and rogues, landowners, merchants, craftsmen, soldiers and slaves, all of whom had their respective ambitious masters. Hammurabi's greatness lies not only in his successful wars and conquests of many lands and their unprecedented administrative demands which were successfully met, but especially in his laws. Before embarking upon his military exploits, he codified the laws of Urukagina of Lagash, Ur-Nammu and others of ancient Sumer, to which he added his own celebrated, liberal laws, all of which took special care to emphasise the protection of the weak and the unprivileged against those with wealth and power; they regulated social relationships and created confidence in the integrity of genuine members of the commercial world. Safety of travel to distant places within the empire encouraged not only business transactions but also the exchange and development of ideas between peoples of foreign lands.

Under King Hammurabi, three social classes are mentioned: the 'man', or upper class; the 'subject' – merchants, traders and the like; the 'slave', on whose backs as always, the structure of society is built. 'Slave' defines someone in thrall – the character of the appellation changes with the times, with very little difference in status, such as serfs in the Middle Ages of Europe, or servants and factory workers in Victorian times and the lowest stratum of workers today. The condition of most slaves of the ancient world was certainly incomparably better than the workers in the cotton fields of America and the factories of nineteenth century Europe. A slave could challenge his master in the courts, if he dared. He could own property and engage in business, provided it did not interfere with his duties to his master. A slave could even buy freedom, either by paying an agreed price, or by marrying a free person.

Hammurabi's codification of his predecessors's laws and his own additions to them, clarified the social disciplines of the land and facilitated their enforcement. Some of his most fundamental social laws correspond with those of Moses, which the Jews received some 500 years later (c.1200). But unlike the Tablets of Moses, Hammurabi's laws have survived to this day, on several plaques of stone or bronze. Many of them are inscribed on a basalt stele 2.25 m. high, in 49 vertical columns, copies of which were to be seen in many parts of the kingdom. It is an important document, properly presented, with a prologue, corpus and epilogue which gives us an insight into the way of life in those remote times.

A very few examples of the Laws in his realm, which were enforced in public courts, might include: an offence against a member of the upper class was considered more serious than against a member of either of the other groups. Can we deny that this is only too often the case within our own society, albeit in disguised forms? A member of the aristocracy was expected to pay more for a given service than a merchant, while a slave need pay nothing at all, and he would still benefit from the service, if it were essential for him to have it.

Women were largely at a disadvantage in a male-dominated society, as indeed they have been (and often still are) in our own society. For the stronger in all aspects of life, very often takes advantage of the weaker. However, in Babylon, although the wife was confined to the home, she had a number of enforceable rights. Marriage, a legally binding institution, gave the woman a sense of security; but if, for example, she was barren and the man wished to divorce her, he had to return her bridal gift and her dowry, before sending her back to her parents. If a husband absconded without making proper provision for his wife, and she then went to live with another man, she did not have to return to her husband when he came back.

A husband could have as many concubines as he could afford. A concubine was usually chosen from the household servants and slaves. If she bore him a son and the father declared: 'You are my son', that would legitimise him and would entitle him to a share in the man's estate. Indulgence of lust was held to contribute to the physical as well as to the spiritual well-being of the citizen. The 'romantic' concept of love, a medieval, European ideal, demands creative activities for its sublimation. The Babylonians do not appear to have had such inhibitions. While Hammurabi's Code does appear to protect the potentially weaker members of society – women, children, slaves – and regulates commercial transactions, thus demonstrating Babylon as a highly civilized society, it would be unrealistic to compare it with modern Western society or even with the social patterns of intervening periods. Each organisation emerges from its predecessor, but the whole is based upon, and ultimately evolved out of the Sumero-Babylonian epoch. Some Babylonian laws seen by us as ideal principles are seldom practised by us: legally setting fair interest rates, fixing prices and wages, both of which prevented exploitation of the weak by temple priests or great land owners.

By 1792, in the reign of Hammurabi, private capital, including land, was a dominant factor in the economy. Thousands of Akkadian documents show business deals, estate accounts, administrative affairs and land sales. Private capital had introduced a revolutionary economic situation which foreshadowed the authority of Babylon as a world power, based upon trade and commerce which had to be regulated. There was an unexpected sophistication in commercial practice. Babylonian goods could be 'paid for' in advance by a promissory note or bill of exchange in Babylonia, on behalf of a customer in the north, to whom the goods would then be transported; there was a market for 'futures' – the coming season's corn could be bought in advance at current price by an astute merchant, who expected a poor crop, which would cause an increase over the current price, to his advantage.

As to agriculture and trade, these had been essential occupations from the earliest times. The production of crops of barley and smaller quantities of wheat, root crops and fruit for man and beast took precedence over all other activities. Wages were paid in kind. As populations grew and cities multiplied, canals for irrigation were extended. Their care and regular inspection was undoubtedly the most important duty of the state. Fresh meat and fish were available in abundance. The great rivers carried merchants and trade from the Gulf to the heart of Anatolia as well as, by a brief portage at the summit of the Fertile Crescent, to Alalakh and the river Orontes, and so to the important Mediterranean ports of Poseideïon, Ugarit, Byblos.

PUBLIC BUILDINGS, such as temples and palaces, had stone foundations, and suitable stones were imported either from the north or the east. Timber was very scarce, the native timber being mainly overgrown fruit trees and the lightweight, date palm, poplar and willow. Heavy tree trunks were available from the foothills of the Zagros mountains, and from Anatolia, they were floated down the two great rivers, much as practised today in Canada and elsewhere. Ordinary people's homes were usually built with mud-brick or clay around an open courtyard, where the family could rest after the day's work. That principle of the open court, surrounded by buildings has continued in the form of caravanserai in the orient and blocks of flats surrounding a green patch for the restful pursuits of city-dwellers in the West.

Elam, a powerful kingdom over the river Karun to the east of Sumer, was for many centuries feared and confronted with varying fortunes by the Mesopotamian kings down to its destruction by Assyria, in the seventh century BC. Yet, it was an effective buffer state against the wild peoples beyond the eastern mountains who coveted the riches of the glittering cities. In the Elamites' successful wars against Babylon, they had carried away from the Temple of Marduk to their capital, Susa (c.1160), Hammurabi's basalt stele inscribed with his laws and Naram-Sin's marvellous statuary depicting him as a conqueror, warrior-king. These were discovered by French archaeologists and are now exhibited at the Louvre, Paris.

Hammurabi, having consolidated his Mesopotamian heritage, evicted the Elamites from the south and successfully confronted the new Semitic power of Assyria in the north. By occupying its capital cities of Ashur and Nineveh, he became the unchallengeable master of the whole of Mesopotamia and peripheral but important city states, such as Mari and Ebla, which gave him access to the Mediterranean. In the manner of the ancient kings, he listed his conquests, twenty four cities, taking away their gods and humiliating their worshippers.

Medical science, as we understand the expression, was non-existent. Certain maladies could be cured by empirical methods. Inevitably, there was, as in primitive societies today, the man or woman who claimed to cure the malady by magic or by conjuring various good spirits. There were diviners who in a few genuine cases, could invoke the hidden (because unused) psychical attributes which living things, including human beings, are said to possess, and might be available for certain purposes. But, in more practical and familiar terms, recent archaeological discoveries of scholarly translations and interpretations, have revealed prescriptions for remedies, involving lists of plants, temperature, frequency of dose, and so forth. Eventually they did differentiate magic from reality:

> Insofar as the texts are in any way revealing of the nature and extent of Babylonian medical practice, they show a level of typical herbal medicine dependent upon an extensive pharmacopoeia and including a number of drugs of known medicinal value. They reveal too the recognition and treatment of a wide variety of diseases . . . . The Code of Hammurabi tells us, however, that surgical operations were performed and that surgeons were skilled in setting broken bones. [3]

However, Babylonians must be credited with the accumulation and development of a prodigious knowledge of astronomy and mathematics. The latter was derived from their Sumerian predecessors, whose knowledge and skills are demonstrated by their monumental architecture – palaces and temples – and their canal-building skills. The Babylonian arithmetical base was hexametric.

> There are tables for multiplying and dividing and for calculating squares and square roots, cubes and cube roots, reciprocals, exponential functions, the sum of square and cubes needed for the numerical solution of certain types of cubic equations, and so forth . . . there existed also a great variety of documents concerned with the formulation and solution of algebraic or geometric problems.[4]

The Pythagorean theorem was often used in the ancient world – in Babylonia as well as in Egypt, long before Pythagoras. The Babylonians replaced the unpredictable length of the lunar month by a civil calendar of twelve months of thirty days. This was necessary for commercial transactions, such as the calculations of interest on loans since it provides a uniform dating method which could be adopted internationally.

They divided the day into twelve by means of the 'shadow clock' or gnomon, which later inspired the construction of the sundial. Herodotus (II.109) recorded

Figure 20. Boundary stone with King Marduk-nadin-ahhe beneath divine symbols and cuneiform inscription. Babylonian, from southern Iraq. (c. 1100 BC). Courtesy, Trustees of the British Museum.

that 'the sun-dial and the gnomon, with the division of the day in twelve parts were received by the Greeks from the Babylonians.'

New light was thrown on Halley's comet in 1985 when reference to it was discovered on a Babylonian cuneiform tablet of 164 BC in the British Museum by Dr Richard Stephenson and Dr K K C Yau, of Durham University and Dr Hermann Hunger of the University of Vienna, and reported in the Scientific journal *Nature*. Although the comet's period – the interval between its close approaches to the earth – is known with some accuracy in recent times, historical records are sparse. The Babylonian reference is the first important addition to the known history of the comet and fills an important gap since no other record of the 164 BC visit is known.

The reference also demonstrates that the Babylonians kept accurate records of comets (another one of its appearance was recorded by the Babylonians in 87 BC), a discovery which may enable scientists to define more precisely than at present how the comet's orbit has changed with time.

Such discoveries enable scientific historians to calculate earlier visits with greater accuracy, which in turn means that even earlier records can be searched specifically for references.[5]

They were dedicated mathematicians, astronomers and scientists, who sought out and resolved problems, not necessarily for any immediate practical purpose, but for the sake of knowledge. In mathematics the Babylonians surpassed the Egyptians. The Greeks became their debtors.

Hammurabi's death in 1750 marks the end of a glorious epoch, for his successors were nonentities. In 1595, the Hittite king Mursili (1620-1595) made a lightning raid on the city of Babylon, looted it, and laid it in ashes, bringing to an end the First Dynasty of the Babylonian Empire. He hastened back to his capital, Hattusa, to crush a palace revolution, where he was himself assassinated. (see chapter 7).

The devastation of the great, ancient city brought social and political chaos in its train, and opened the way for its seizure and occupation by the Sealander-Sumerians, for an as yet unknown period. The name 'Sealanders' describes a dynasty of Ur which appeared after the death of Hammurabi, ruling a distinct area in the marshlands, south of Babylon, occupying a territory which included the ancient Sumerian cities of holy Nippur and temporal Eridu. The region was a seat of learning and culture. Towards the end of its historical period (c.1559) it included even the city of Babylon itself. Interspersed within the general realignment of historical continuity, there appeared the Gutians, who have already been described above. They were ousted by Ur-Nammu, the founder of the Third Dynasty of Ur (c. 2000). Very little seems to be known of that period. It is, therefore, dubbed 'the Dark Ages'.

THE KASSITES (c. 1595 - c. 1161) This people had been infiltrating Babylonia for a century or more from the direction of the Zagros Mountains. Their language seems to contain elements which, if really Aryan, are perhaps among the oldest traces of the Indo-European speech (c.1800). They expelled the Sealanders and remained masters of Babylonia for 400 years. They could be described as the vanguard of the great Aryan hordes which ultimately occupied and established their own kingdoms in the vast territories east of the Tigris – the kingdoms of the Medes and the Persians (Parsua) being the most important.

The Kassites seem to have been rather an unimaginative people; not creative, but, as time proved, manifestly good administrators. However, if they had no contribution to make to the high Babylonian culture, they at least recognised, appreciated, preserved and adopted for themselves the immense wealth of knowledge, the traditions and even the Semitic language and religion of their subjects; so much so that, but for the written sources of their strange names, they might have been confounded with their Babylonian Semitic predecessors.

They had overrun the southern Sumerian-Sealand territories by 1460 and thus created an homogeneous kingdom of Babylonia from the Gulf northwards towards Assyria and Ashur. There must have been a struggle for supremacy between Kassites and Sealanders for about 100 years, before the Kassites prevailed (c.1495). They proved to be diplomatic rulers: they restored the original temples and public buildings of Sumer, before raising new buildings of their own, in the ancient Sumerian cities of Ur, Eridu, Uruk and elsewhere. They were liberal, unoppressive and even more successful administrators of their huge kingdom than their Babylonian and Akkadian predecessors. They adopted so much of Babylonian culture and so many of its institutions that the continuity of ancient Babylon under the Kassites remained almost seamless, and Kassite-Babylon often continued to be referred to as 'Babylon' or 'Babylonia'. That period could be described as 'the Kassite Dynasty of Babylon', which came to an end c.1157 (see chapter 9).

These were critical times, indeed. The stability which the Babylonian Empire represented in and around Mesopotamia, was ruined after the death of Hammurabi by the destructive invasion of the Hittite King Mursili, the emergence of the Sealanders from the south, and the appearance and threat of a new Aryan people, the Mitanni in the north. The usurpation of the Babylonian inheritance by the Kassites restored the stability of that Kingdom.

Kassite diplomacy dictated friendship with Egypt. Pharaoh Ahmosis, founder of the 18th Dynasty, had expelled the Hyksos (c.1560), and the Egyptian kings were making forays into Palestine-Syria. They were confronted by the powerful northern kingdom of Mitanni and the Hittites. But the Egyptian Amarna Letters, mainly from Pharaohs Amunhotep III and Akhenaten's reigns (c.1402-1347) (see chapter 5), contain correspondence with the Babylonian (Kassite) monarchs, Kadashman-Enlil I (c.1370) and Burnaburiash II (c.1350), who are addressed as 'brother', indicating an equal royal status. That political friendship facilitated the journeys of the Babylonian caravans of merchandise to and from Syria, Egypt and Anatolia. There is evidence of trade even with Greece in the fourteenth century, as witnessed by 'a Mycenaean "ox-hide" ingot at Dur-Kurigalzu and Kassite seals in Greece (Thebes)'.[6] Valuable royal gifts were exchanged and a cordial diplomatic relationship appears to have existed. There is even an amusing passage in which Amunhotep II teases his ambassador for his romantic escapades with ladies of every class and age, in every city he visited on matters of State.[7]

This happy state of affairs was already declining early in the fourteenth century, especially as Assyria began to show signs of independence during the reign of its king Ashur-ubalit (1365-1330) by opening up direct relationship with Tutankhamun's Egypt, much to the displeasure and concern of Babylon's Burnaburiash II, who had treated the Assyrian king as an upstart. But the marriage of the Assyrian's daughter with the Babylonian crown prince, and the latter's ascension to the Babylonian throne after his father's death, brought with it many political complications, which were to tie the fortunes of the two powers together, until Assyrian might frightened Babylon into seeking an alliance with the Hittites (c. 1290).

Towards the end of the thirteenth century Assyria's king Tukulti-Ninurta I (1244-1208), raided Babylon, sacked it, and made the Babylonian king prisoner. He could then call himself 'Lord of Sumer-Akkad' in its entirety and boast that his land was bounded by the Lower Sea in the south. This was a physical death but a cultural victory for Kassite-Babylon, in the same sense as the Roman occupation of Greece made the Romans more Greek than the Greeks themselves in their desire to become the cultural heirs of the ancient people.

At the end of the thirteenth century, the appearance of the Sea and Land Peoples – nomads, pirates, wild peoples, invaders and destroyers of established kingdoms, was to change the political face of the whole of the civilized world (see chapter 8). Thenceforth, Assyrian military power increasingly dominates the historical stage of the Near East.

Notes

1. Dower Margaret S., *Syria Before 2200 BC*, CAH I², p. 321.
2. Oates Joan, *Babylon*, Thames & Hudson, London, 1979, p. 37.
3. Oates Joan, *Babylon*, Thames & Hudson, London, 1979, pp. 182-3.

4. Ibid, pp. 184-5.
5. Tucker Anthony, *The Guardian*, 19 April 1985 (abridged).
6. Oates Joan, Babylon, op cit. p. 91.
7. Brinkman, J.A., 1972, AJA 76, 274, quoted by Joan Oates, op. cit. p. 88.

Authors Note – The Ayran group of languages from remote prehistoric times, originated in northern India and Afghanistan (Bactria, Sogdiana). It is usually (misleadingly) called *Indo-European* because most European languages stem from it. When referring to any one of that group of languages I have used Indo-European, Indo-Ayran of Ayran to describe them.

Chapter 4
The Jews

Earlier I referred to the explosion of the Semitic peoples from the Arabian desert. They appeared on the littoral of the Mediterranean, the regions we know as Palestine and Syria, in search of fresh pastures for their animals and corn for themselves. A tribe of Canaanites, the Arameans, established themselves astride the commercial crossroads of eastern and northern Syria including the great port of Ugarit. They became skilled in handling caravan traffic. Other Canaanites we recognise as the Phoenicians, from as far back as the third millennium BC, were the founders of great sea-ports such as Tyre and Aradus, both attached to islands, Sidon, Byblos and Berytus. As a result of their trading relations with Egypt, Crete and ultimately with all the Levantine lands, as well as peoples far beyond the Levant, they became prosperous seafarers. Those ports of course also became the *entrepôts*, for the caravans laden with goods of Mesopotamian merchants, which reached the Mediterranean via the Fertile Crescent and returned to their homelands laden with stocks of imported goods. After the destruction of Philistine sea and land power by King David of Israel (c .975), the Phoenicians became a maritime power. They were a link between nations with an almost complete monopoly of international commerce. From the tenth century there were Phoenician merchants in Cyprus and Sardinia exploiting the mineral wealth of those islands. They then sailed to Spain and north Africa. Carthage, founded in 810 BC, became an empire in its own right. This was the apogee of Phoenician wealth and power. At the end of the seventh century BC, in the reign of Pharaoh Necho II, a small canal was dug between the eastern arm of the Nile and the head of the Gulf of Suez whence a squadron of Phonecian sailors succeeded in circumnavigating Africa from east to west in three years. Later (sixth century BC) Hanno the Carthaginian was unsuccessful in achieving the same feat in the opposite direction. He sailed from Carthage via the Straits of Gibraltar and down the west coast of Africa. He reached Gambia and somewhat beyond, before returning to Carthage. Phoenician command of the Straits of Gibraltar obliged the Greeks, whose commander, Massila, had founded Marseilles, to find a route along the Rhone to northern France and so to the tin mines of Cornwall (c. 500 BC). The Phoenicians are said to have exploited those mines, but this is doubtful.

The demotic version of the Egyptian hieroglyphics had been introduced by

Figure 21. Ivory openwork plaque with a seated lion wearing an Egyptian pectoral and sun-disc. From Nimrud (Calah). Phoenician c. 850BC, ht 13.6 cm. Courtesy, Trustees of the British Museum.

the Egyptians at Byblos (the town that inspired the noun 'book', the Bible being *the* book). Soon after 1500, that version was adapted by the Phoenicians for an alphabet of 22 simple consonants (vowels were not used) which could be written on papyrus. It was ultimately adopted by the Greeks who added vowels, and the complete sequence of letters was eventually taken up by Rome and transmitted to Western Europe.

The foregoing is a passing glimpse the history of the Canaanites in Palestine. Other Semites continued northwards along the Fertile Crescent and founded great cities such as Ebla and Mari. Yet others went southwards, along the valley of the Euphrates, in the manner of nomads and tent dwellers and moved about with their possessions of sheep and goats and donkey caravans from place to place in search of pastures, in accordance with seasonal changes or the prospect of acquiring wealth by attacking weak city-states or founding others themselves, *en route*.

Such were the peoples known as the 'Apiru', person from across and beyond.
. . which recurs in cuneiform texts from different parts of Mesopotamia, Syria, Egypt and Asia Minor, all dating between the Dynasty of Akkad (2234-2154) and the eleventh century BC. [1]

'Apiru' is identified by some scholars with Abraham. At the end of the Dynasty of Akkad (c.2154) and again after about 1800, there were violent political, social and consequential disruptions of caravaneering, and the donkey caravaneers were forced into other occupations in order to exist.

THE JEWS. Yet other Semites, the Jews, later came to live in the land of Canaan. Theirs is a stormy history because of the geographical position of their country which bestrides the highway between Egypt, Syria, Anatolia and Mesopotamia. During the long wars between the great powers of Egypt and Assyria, the Jews had difficulty in maintaining their independence. In this outline of the history of a vast geographical region, where great kingdoms arose and, sooner or later, disappeared, a whole chapter has been devoted to the history of a small, almost insignificant Semitic people – the Jews. Although neither the territorial extent of their homeland, their numbers, nor their military achievements are of any moment, it is their God, Yahveh or Jehovah who has been adopted by a majority of the world's population, whose religious teachers, Jesus and Mohammed, go hand

in hand with the Jewish Moses in preaching the Word of God, the Father.

The story of the Jews has a long, legendary beginning, from which the historical period eventually emerges. The Old Testament, the main source for the early period, wholly pertains to the Jews. It includes the stories of the Pentateuch, the first 'Five Books', large portions of which are said to have been written by Moses and added to, almost certainly, by Joshua after the death of Moses (c.1200).

> The entity Israel, though probably prepared by a much older national religious team-spirit of some tribes or tribal groups which later merged into 'Israel', was first created by David (c.980), and thereafter continued to exist at least as an ideal, an object of desire for which man strove. In view of this idea, 'all Israel', all those groups and individual personalities of the time before Moses who were remembered thereafter, were given enlarged dimensions, quite as a matter of course. They were treated as precursors of the Israel which David had created, not simply of particular parts of it. This had widespread effects, one of which was that it became necessary to place these personalities in a genealogical succession.[2]

The name 'Israel' was first used by Pharaoh Meneptah (c.1200).

What follows is mainly the Biblical version of the history, with occasional comments. It is therefore necessary to keep firmly in mind the above introductory paragraphs: that 'Israel' is an emotive name used by King David, to describe the various independent tribes who had become his subjects. The idea of 'Israel' and the 'One God' gave his people a sense of unity. The names of the patriarchs, after Abraham – Isaac, Jacob, Joseph – might well represent separate nomadic tribes which were personified under those names – eponyms. By such personification, a hierarchy was invented which gave credence to Abraham and his 'progeny', and continuity to the story of 'Israel', the name given by God to Jacob (Gen.XXXII.28).

Abraham and his clan appeared as tent dwellers in the vicinity of Ur, around 1900 BC. Perhaps he was born there. He must have lived in that region for a long time, for on comparing some Biblical texts with certain Sumero-Akkadian legends, one feels justified in surmising that he absorbed certain aspects of the ethos and traditions of his birthplace. He must have heard of, accepted and transmitted to his descendants, the Sumerian *Gilgamesh* stories of the Creation and the Great Flood. Then, in the manner of nomads, he moved north up the Euphrates valley to Harran (perhaps a city of the Hurrites (see chapter 7)), on his way to Canaan. Passing by Akkad, he would have learnt the story of the origin of King Sargon the Great and how, as a baby, he was found in a basket, lined with bitumen, on the banks of a river – a tradition with which much later, Moses was clothed. The tabernacle was a fixed or movable habitation usually of slight construction; 'Feast of the Tabernacle' describes the Jewish autumn festival commemorating the dwelling of the Jews in the wilderness. A tent was used as a sanctuary.

At Harran, Abraham's grandson, Jacob, seeks the hand in marriage of Laban's daughter, Rachel, and stays behind to labour for Laban for seven years as a condition for marrying her. But Laban breaks his word and forces Jacob to marry his eldest daughter, Leah, and to work for yet another seven years for his consent to marry his second daughter, Rachel, as well. This is a story taken from cuneiform tablets discovered in the ancient city of Nuzi (east of the Tigris, near modern Kirkuk) which reveal to us, perhaps, Hurrite or Hurrian traditions and rules of marriage and inheritance, some of which were adopted by the Jews, as described in the Old Testament (Gen. XXIX). Jacob had ten sons by Leah, and two sons, Joseph and Benjamin, by Rachel, who became the founders of the Twelve Tribes of Israel.

Abraham and his household departed from Harran, following the Fertile Crescent, towards Canaan. He, his clan and possessions – asses, sheep, goats – seem to have wandered between Egypt and Palestine and finally settled in Canaan. Again, dipping into the pages of the Old Testament (Gen.XVI), Abraham's wife, Sara, we are told was barren. Therefore, in accordance with the custom of those times, she tells Abraham to 'go in unto my maid (Hagar)'. Hagar bears Abraham a son, Ishmael. This takes place 'in the land of Canaan'. To assuage the distress of Hagar in the face of Sara's jealousy, who had in the meantime given birth to Isaac, God promises the maid that He 'will multiply her seed exceedingly.' He does so. The Ishmaelites are the Arabians who claim Abraham as their founding father, through Ishmael, in the land of Canaan or Palestine which they on the one hand and the Jews on the other, assert is their own God-given homeland. Hence, to some extent, the current troubles in Palestine. Today, Hagar and Ishmael lie on one side of the Kaaba in Mecca.

On the religious side, God, as he is presented to us in the Bible, is not without competitors. 'There is the story about the change in Jacob's name to Israel, which occurred at Penuel or Bethel' (Gen.XXXII.29; XXXV.10), and another story that he gave the name 'El, god of Israel to an altar erected at Shechem. It is possible that (as Gen.XXXII.29; XXXII.20, seem to show) the name Isra-El was accepted by the Jacob group in connection with the acceptance of the worship of El.'[3]

The story of Joseph is, very possibly, yet another historical event of primary importance, which has taken on the mantle of legend. He (the eponymous leader of his tribe) was taken in captivity to Egypt, where he rose to be a high-ranking official, and eventually, during a widespread famine, helped his brothers (and their people), who had betrayed him. Here, it is proposed that it was the motley nomadic people, known as the Hyksos (see chapter 5, *Egypt*), who took Joseph and his tribe prisoner or accepted them into their ranks (c.1700 BC), before infiltrating Egypt. Therefore, eventually as allies of the Hyksos or 'Shepherd kings of Egypt', the Jews found freedom and success in the Delta region. Other Israelites, through Joseph's good offices, had been given the land of Goshen, within Egypt. Joseph's own preferment at court personified the general well-being of his tribe. The true Egyptian Pharaohs were driven south where they ruled from Thebes.

The Hyksos were expelled from Egypt by the true pharaohs in the sixteenth century BC. Without their friendly rulers, in a foreign land, the Jews were regarded and treated as slaves. They must have been in Egypt for about 300 years, until the thirteenth century BC. If so, then, among other Pharaonic masters, they would also have been under the rule of the enlightened Pharaoh Amunhotep IV, better known as Akhenaten (1379-1362). He and his beautiful queen, Nefertiti, denied their own traditional gods, and introduced the monotheistic cult of Aten, the Sun-god (see chapter 5, *Egypt*). It would have been difficult for a small group of subject people to resist taking part in the worship and temple-ceremonies of the monotheistic Pharaoh's new and only god, Akhenaten's reign of nearly 20 years must surely have left its imprint on most of the people in Egypt, including the Jews.

Traditionally, it was in the reign of Rameses II (1304-1237) that Moses, born of Jewish, Levite parents, in the service of Pharaoh's daughter, and sympathetic to the Jewish sufferings, led them away, ultimately beyond Pharaoh's reach. During their wanderings in the desert, 'Moses married the daughter of a Midianite (Arab) priest who worshipped Yahveh (Jehovah), a north Arabian desert deity, originally a moon-god, whose abode was a tent and whose ritual comprised feasts and sacrifices.'[4] Her name was Zipporah (Ex.II.21). But, in our times, in 1981, Dr. Hans Goedicke, a respected Egyptologist, Chairman of the Department of Near Eastern Studies at Johns Hopkins University, Baltimore, offered a theory which puts Exodus back to the year 1477 BC, in the reign of Pharaoh-Queen Hatshepsut, 200 years before the traditional time of the Flight.[5] That would make it impossible to link Jewish monotheism to that of Akhenaten (c.1379-1362). There still remained the influence of the Midianite wife of Moses who might well have induced him to accept her own tribe's only (or chief) God, Yahveh or Jehovah.

That possibility also gives some credibility to 'the waters were divided' (Exodus XIV.21) for the crossing of the Jews. That 'miracle' would have happened perhaps during the prodigious eruption of the volcanic mountain on the Isle of Thera, which destroyed the Minoan civilization in Crete and, by all accounts, sent shock-waves to far-away lands and influenced the whole world climatically or in some other way. Such a shock to relatively nearby Egypt, might well have disrupted the normal state of the Red Sea which briefly might have overflowed into the surrounding lands and thus created a passage for the crossing of the fugitive Jews. The Bible story confirms the atmospheric conditions caused by such an eruption – 'a cloud of darkness' which 'gave light by night' perhaps by gigantic flames emanating from the bursting mountain, appearing over the distant horizon.

Then, Moses received the Tablet containing the Ten Commandments. Faced with the wilfulness and perversity of his people, he smashed it in despair. It was made of clay, so there is no trace of it now. But Hammurabi's laws (eighteenth century BC) engraved on stone or bronze plaques, have survived to this day. The

Ten Commandments have important affinities with the Laws of Hammurabi. Hence, even if the original Tablet of Moses is not available, the Ten Commandments, as implied by Hammurabi's version and reproduced in the Old Testament, are traditional, fundamental rules of life, which have had a disciplinary and salutary influence upon the behaviour of its adherents. 'The Ark' was a wooden coffer containing tables of the Jewish Laws, including the Ten Commandments. At this stage, legend gives place to history – *Exodus*: The tribesmen wandered for many years in Sinai, the Negeb and the Trans-Jordan deserts, until c.1230. Then, led by Joshua, they (about 7,000 of them) appeared around the peripheries of the petty kingdoms of Edom, Moab and Ammon, obviously making for the fertile land of Canaan.

They conquered Jericho, burnt down Hazor (capital of several city states) infiltrated and intermarried with the Semitic Canaanites generally. It is from such a fusion that the ancestors of the Jews were descended. They were also reunited with their cousins, Jacob's progeny by Leah, representing ten tribes and the Benjamites, who had not been in Egypt. The land was divided into eleven parts, one for each tribe. The twelfth tribe, that of the priestly Levites, was dispersed among its brethren, in order to minister to their religious needs. Settled at last in the fertile lands of Canaan, the Jews went through a number of developing phases: the priestly Judges were followed by the Prophets, and up to the time of Samuel, they seem to have been content to be ruled by their prophets in times of war and peace.

A completely new threat suddenly appeared (c.1190) from overseas: the Philistines, an Aryan people, invaded the Palestine littoral and threatened the independence of the peoples of Canaan (see chapter 8). Their strength lay in their knowledge of the complicated process of smelting iron, and in manufacturing iron weapons of war. Their attempt to invade Egypt (perhaps from Crete) had been frustrated by Rameses III (1198-1166) with whom they came to terms (1188) and he gave them lands, including Gaza, where they could settle down, in return for military service. By c.1175, they had become very powerful and in time extended their territory beyond Gaza, on the coastal plain between the mountains of Jordan and the sea. Thus, to the despair of the Jews, their country was cut in half.

Then the Jews clamoured for a king who would lead them against their enemy, conquer new lands and give them material wealth. The prophet Samuel had to comply with their demand. He anointed Saul and declared him to be the first king of the Jews (c.1015-1000). Saul united the small chieftainships into a single kingdom, went to war against the Philistines and was sorely defeated at the battle of Mount Gilboa. His army fled and 'Saul took a sword and fell upon it and when the Philistines found him, they cut off his head, put his armour in the temple of Ashtaroth; and they fastened his body to the wall at Beth-Shean.' (1 Samuel XXXI abridged).

It was not until the time of David (c.1000-960), successor of Saul, that the process of smelting iron and its application for the manufacture of iron implements became generally known. David, King of Judaea, in the seventh year of his reign, seized the independent city of Jerusalem, successfully invaded the northern state of Israel and became ruler of both states as 'King of Israel'. Having broken Philistine power, with his new iron weapons of war, he gave Israel a sense of nationality. The Philistines, a foreign, uncircumcised element in a Semitic region, disappeared after David's reign, perhaps absorbed into the native Semitic populations, with little trace of their origin or culture.

David implemented an important commercial and political alliance with King Hiram of Tyre (Phoenicia) which put his country on the international political stage. He realised the significance of literature, religious poetry and music and patronised them. Israeli archaeologists, directed by Dr Yigal Shiloh of the Hebrew University, discovered, in 1979, the site of King David's Biblical capital of 3000 years ago in Jerusalem. The main dig along the eastern slopes of Mount Ophal uncovered the remains of David's and his son Solomon's cities.

Solomon (c 960-930) continued his father's policy of friendship not only with Phoenician Tyre, but also with other neighbouring countries through extension of trading relationships. His own cargo boats laden with goods, sailed off from Aqaba. He encouraged the development of agriculture and the exploitation of mines. He built an impressive royal palace and a great temple; there was lavish entertainment and there were many marriages. The stories of his splendours and his huge harem are mostly true, although his fame for wisdom and justice cannot be substantiated. Most of his foreign wives did not recognise Jehovah, the Jewish God, and, in old age, he was prevailed upon by them to make sacrifices to their own idols; an indication of loss of personal and national prestige. The Temple of Solomon was probably built in the tenth century BC and destroyed by the Babylonians in 586. (see chapter 9).

The far-famed Queen of Sheba. we are told, sailed up the Red Sea in her sumptuous, royal barge, to visit him, and, if so, trading treaties must have been made between the two monarchs. Tradition has it that she bore him a son who became the founder of the royal house of Ethiopia. This traditional version has been questioned by a Belgian priest and archaeologist, Father Albert Jamme, a professor at the Catholic University in Washington, DC, during his preparation for 'an expedition to Marib, the 3000-year-old walled city on the edge of the Arabian desert which, with its huge dam, has always been regarded as the jewel of the Queen of Sheba's long-lost realm.'

According to Father Jamme 'the Queen of Sheba' did not even live in the fabled land of Sheba – Saba in the Yemen. Traditionally, the Queen of Sheba is believed to have been an ancestor of the Ethiopian emperor. Father Jamme discovered that in Ethiopia she is called Queen Maqweda. He is convinced that 'Maqweda', a proper name, is a mistranslation of the Arabic word *maqtuwiat* or chieftain. Therefore the 'Queen' Sheba would have been no more than the chieftain of a small tribe in the north-west corner of Saudi Arabia. Why, then all the fuss about 'Queen Sheba' visiting King Solomon? 'Simple,' says Father Jamme. 'Solomon was really a very small king. The Old Testament propagandists played up the importance of Sheba to boost Solomon's reputation.'[6]

Solomon's extravagance created public discontent and resulted in the division of the nation and a struggle between his sons for the succession, after his death. The problem was resolved by reverting to the original two states: Israel in the north and Judaea in the south, with their capitals respectively at Samaria and Jerusalem. In c.930 Pharaoh Shishak captured Jerusalem and carried away the treasures of the temple of Solomon.

Ahab of the House of Omri, king of Israel (874-853) married, through his father's (Omri's) diplomacy, the Phoenician princess, Jezebel, daughter of the powerful Tyrian priest-king, Ethball. Her corruptive influence broke the old faith which had sustained the Jews through so many difficult situations. The Israelites increasingly assimilated the ways and even the gods of their neighbours, with many intermarriages, which eventually almost expunged Jewish traditions. Ahab, by his marriage, reaped the benefits of parental statesmanship. It was Ahab who provided Syria with 2,000 chariots and 10,000 infantry and checked the advance of Shalmaneser III of Assyria at Qarqar (c.853). He died in battle against the Aramaeans (c.853).

Jehu, commander of the Israelite army, encouraged by the prophet Elisha, who cried out against the pagan court-religions introduced by the queen-mother, Jezebel, led a successful *coup d'état* and was anointed king by the prophet. All the conservative elements in court and country united against the House of Omri. When the true kings of Israel and Judaea came to make peace with Jehu they were assassinated and the bloody purges that followed had few parallels in the history of the Jews. Jehu then claimed a spurious membership of the royal house of Omri. He was involved in many wars with neighbouring city-states, but the most terrible enemy to confront was Shalmaneser III, king of Assyria (860-825). In the face of the new, fearful danger, Jehu and Syria-Aramaea buried old rivalries and survived the enemy's first and second assaults. However, at the third onslaught, Jehu abandoned his allies and submitted. The detailed carvings on the famous Black Obelisk of basalt, about six feet high, exhibited at the British Museum are eloquent of the submission of the Israelites, showing Jehu on his knees, with bowed head touching the ground at Shalmaneser's feet. Among many other carvings, Assyrians are depicted carrying away the defeated enemy's treasure.

During the reigns of the two weak successors of Shalmaneser, Israel's Jeroboam II and Judaea's Uzziah (822-783) extended their respective territories, occupying Damascus and Trans-Jordan in the north and Philistine lands on the coast. They reached a level of prosperity and wealth which exceeded the glories of Solomon. The prophets cried out against the greed and abuse of power of the upper classes. But, by the end of the first half of the eighth century, the dormant reciprocal jealousies between the two small Jewish kingdoms had risen to mutual hatred. Judaea was so blinded by it as to invite the Assyrian king, Tiglath-Pileser III (Pul,2 Kings XV.19) (745-727) for assistance against Israel, her rival. The upshot was that Israel became a tributary of Assyria. In 722 Sargon II (722-705) destroyed Israel, and deported its noblemen and young men: 'I conquered Samaria and led away 27,270 inhabitants. I rebuilt and settled in the new town people from other foreign lands I had conquered.' The remaining Israelites mingled with immigrant Assyrians and Babylonians, ultimately to form the tiny community of the Samaritans.

Judaea survived for 115 years beyond Israel, but only as a tribute-paying appendage of the mighty Assyrian Empire. After Assyria's destruction in 607, Judaea was invaded by Nebuchadnezzar II (587) of the Neo-Babylonian Empire (see chapter 9). Jerusalem was taken by storm and a general massacre of the population followed.

Figure 23. Shalmaneser III, King of Assyria (859-824), receiving the Israelite tribute and the humiliating submission of King Jehu of Israel. Detail from the Black Obelisk. Nimrud, c. 825 BC. Courtesy, Trustees of the British Museum.

And the army of the Chaldees pursued the king (Zedekiah) and overtook him and all his army was scattered. They took Zedekiah to Riblah to the king of Babylon, who gave judgment upon him. And they slew his sons before his eyes, and put out his eyes, and bound him with fetters of brass, and carried him to Babylon. (Paraphrased)

[In Jerusalem] . . . all the vessels and treasures of the house of God, great and small, and the treasure of the king and the princes; all of these he (Nebuchadnezzar) brought to Babylon. And they burnt the house of God and brake down the walls of Jerusalem, and burnt all the palaces thereof with fire. And them that had escaped from the sword carried he away captive to Babylon, where they were servants to him and his sons. (2 Kings XXV).

During their sixty years as a subject, quasi-slave people in Babylon, the Jews returned to the Way of God. The voices of the prophets prevailed, and Babylon's idols were forgotten. In 537 King Cyrus the Great of Persia overran Babylonia and Palestine. He released the Jews and allowed them to return to Jerusalem. Many of them had prospered and preferred to remain in Babylon rather than emigrate to a ruined city, although a new temple had been built and King Cyrus had returned their sacred vessels to Jerusalem.

The Jews reverted to their strict religious beliefs. Their genius for growth in numbers and riches has always brought upon them the vicious jealousy of their neighbours. Henceforth they are under the 'protection' or direct rule of one kingdom or empire after another but they consider themselves, more than ever a people apart from others, 'a chosen people' (as some Christians assume to be 'the elect'). They await the coming of that Leader who will cause nation not to 'rise up against nation' nor 'to learn war any more'.

The traditions of the times and the nature of God were extremely uncertain. God reflects the image of those that worship Him. In the early era He is 'a jealous God'. He curses Adam and Eve and expels them for ever from Paradise; introduces Cain, personifying jealousy and murder; there is deception when Jacob passes himself as Esau; there are many instances of favours for the rich and powerful; the abuse of power and wealth; adultery, even incest, and so forth. Finally, we read of God putting Abraham's faith to trial by ordering him to sacrifice his only son, Isaac. Although at the last moment He intercedes, we are still presented with a God who inspires us with fear, not love. He demands sacrifice, and obedience and utmost faith. The *lex talionis* of the Ten Commandments, an eye for an eye; a tooth for a tooth, does not reflect forgiveness and tolerance, nor

Figure 24. Sargon II king of Assyria (721-705), witnessing the blinding of Zedekiah for treason. After Daniel Rops, Historie Sainte, *Librairie Artheme Fayard, Paris.*

always even justice.

But as the Great Story progresses, as the characters in it come in contact with higher civilizations embodying more sensitive ethical concepts, so the Jewish God takes on a more humane, a more generous image. Isaiah (I.11), at last, speaks with the voice of a softer image (in contrast to the earlier barbaric words) of God, who says:

> To what purpose is the multitude of your sacrifices unto me? I am full of the burnt offerings of rams, and the fat of fed beasts; and I delight not in the blood of bullocks, or of lambs, or he-goats. Your new moons and your appointed feasts my soul hateth. I am weary to bear them. And when you spread forth your hands, I will hide mine eyes from you: yea, when ye make many prayers, I will not hear; your hands are full of blood. Wash you, make yourselves clean; put away the evil of your doings from before mine eyes, cease to do evil; learn to do well.

Then, in the New Testament, Jesus, unrealistically exhorts us to 'turn the other cheek thus shaming one's opponent or enemy to desist. But the teachings of Jesus were those of an idealist, and far in advance of the old Jewish creed, and even 2000 years later, of our own times.

> The world of scholarship acknowledges the stupendous contribution of universal moment, in the form of the Book known as the Bible. It contains histories by objective chroniclers, such as the Books of Samuel and Kings; powerful prose and poetic literature, as found in the Psalms and the Song of Songs; the narratives of Ruth and Esther; the wisdom of Job and Ecclesiastes; the uncompromising monotheism of Amos and Isaiah, the ethical nobility of Jeremiah and Hosea. The importance of the many aspects of the Book lies in the absolute originality and integrity of its contents.[7]

The Hebrews had been a desert people and so they would have remained had they not adopted every aspect of Canaanite culture. They did so: language and alphabet (Phoenician), farming, complete with fertility rites; many adopted the worship of Yahveh's powerful rival, Baal. Art, music, poetry, all came via the Canaanites. Every aspect of secular life was Canaanite. In this moving and remarkable story the prophets play a very important part. They are the oracles and soothsayers who divine 'the word of the Lord' and to whom everyone turns for advice in times of distress. They are leaders who dare face the king and denounce his unrighteous ways and, inspired by 'the word of the Lord', they prophesy events to come; they are the shepherds of a nation.

Notes

1. Albright W.F., 'The Armana Letters from Palestine', *CAH II²*, pp. 111-114.
2. Einsfeldt O., 'Palestine in the Time of the Nineteenth Dynasty', *CAH II²*, pp. 308, 318.
3. Einsfeldt O., *op. cit.* p. 318.
4. Hitti Philip K., *A Short History of Syria*, Macmillan, London, 1959, p. 47.
5. Brummer Alex, reporting from Washington DC in *The Guardian* newspaper, 4 May 1981.
6. Watson Peter, *The Guardian* newspaper.
7. Hitti Philip K., *op. cit.* p. 51.

Chapter 5
Egypt

Egypt's roots go back 10,000 years, to the Pre-dynastic Period, and possibly to earliest man, of whom traces have been found by geologists in the far south, in the vicinity of Lake Rudolf. The river Nile, flowing through thousands of miles of desert, would have attracted nomads settling upon its banks to practise a primitive husbandry, the annual inundations of the river having at first overwhelmed them, destroying their settlements and meagre possessions. The significance of the fertile deposits of silt offered to them by the ebbing waters, was at last seen and understood. Irrigation promoted permanent settlements and communal effort. Villages grew into towns and eventually into two natural regions, Lower and Upper Egypt: Lower Egypt, with its broad delta opening out to the Mediterranean, and Upper Egypt, a long waterway, a fertile corridor flowing from the south through the inhospitable eastern Sahara. A prolonged conflict for supremacy developed between the rulers of the two regions.

It is generally accepted that, of the two civilizations, the Mesopotamian came before that of the Egyptian. While there is ample evidence of Sumerian presence in Egypt around 3100, there is no corresponding, convincing evidence of the converse possibility at that time in Mesopotamia. To reach Egypt from Sumer, early trader-explorers might have sailed up the Euphrates, across to the river Orontes and out into the Mediterranean; followed by a long and hazardous sea journey, hugging the Syria-Palestine coast, to Egypt. Alternatively, caravans could have travelled over the Fertile Crescent, through the wild lands of Syria-Palestine and the burning sands of the Sinai desert. However, many scholars now accept the probability of a dangerous sea voyage, as demonstrated in our times by Thor Heyerdal: out of the Persian Gulf, along the Arabian coast, into the Red Sea. Then, perhaps, up the river (now the wadi) Hammamat, about 300 km above the First Cataract. A knife handle found at Gebel el-Araq (south of Abydos), with foreign ships engraved upon it, gives some native Egyptian credence to this theory.

Monumental architecture, as depicted by the great Pyramids, which even by today's standards represent astonishing building, indeed, engineering and mathematical proficiency of a high order, also stand witness to Sumerian influence. Those buildings appeared not long after 3000. We have only to look and wonder at the beautiful temples and ziggurats of Uruk and Eridu, which date far before

3000 BC, to arrive at the probability of Sumerian instruction which helped the Egyptians so soon after their probable date of arrival, to lay the foundations of their own Egyptian style of architecture, to conform to their own particular needs and traditions.

Similarly, it is possible that it was under Sumerian influence that the native Egyptian writing – the hieroglyphic script – developed over the centuries. Unlike the Mesopotamian, the existence of ancient Egypt and its advanced civilization was never forgotten. Material evidence of the immense pyramids and colossal, columned ruins of palaces and temples stood witness to that civilization. The Bible is rich with references to ancient Egypt. It was in the nineteenth century, when Napoleon invaded Egypt, that scholarly investigations as to its true history began. Napoleon intended to associate his reign with the solution of the Egyptian mystery. He took with him a number of *savants* as well as artists, who copied the engravings and made drawings of the monuments, which were studied and exhibited in France.

The ancient Egyptian writing was found engraved on many of the Egyptian monuments, and painted on walls, coffins and other surfaces, it also appears on pieces of papyri. Three forms of writing may be distinguished: the *hieroglyphic*, a pictorial form; the *hieratic*, a developed, therefore a simplified, form of the hieroglyphic; the *demotic,* a late cursive script. By good fortune the French came upon a basalt slab, the Rosetta Stone, which had three sections of writing on it: the hieroglyphic, cursive Egyptian and Greek. As the Greek could be read it was only a matter of time before the other two sections, of which the Greek was a translation, could also be read. Proper names were enclosed in an oblong circle called a *cartouche.* The script was a decree by the Egyptian priesthood to honour King Ptolemy V (196 BC).

The decipherment of the scripts tried the patience and perseverance of many scholars. The most famous of them, Jean-François Champollion, was born in Fugeac, France in 1790, an extremely talented child. In 1801, three years after Napoleon invaded Egypt with a host of scholars who would penetrate the mysteries of ancient Egypt, Champollion was sent to a school in Grenoble where he took an increasing interest in Hebrew, which was followed with a study of the Coptic language (Ethiopian), which is similar to ancient Egyptian. In 1808 he was shown a copy of the inscriptions on the Rosetta Stone. At first he, like other Egyptologists at the time, thought that the hieroglyphics were symbols and that his efforts to decipher the inscriptions on the stone must be directed to the demotic version. But he realised his mistake when he determined that one hieroglyph represented a phonetic value and that a cartouche (an oval ring) contained a name. The two names which appeared at the base of Cleopatra's Needle, which was erected on the Embankment in London in 1878, were Cleopatra and Ptolemy; the fact that they had the letters l,p,t,o,e in common, helped Champollion to establish that the hieroglyphic system was alphabetic. This is no more than a simplified version of all the learning and effort on the part of Champollion, Thomas Young, William John Bankes and others, which eventually solved the puzzle of ancient Egyptian writing and opened up a vast historical library from the transcripts of the symbols on monuments, coffins of the pharaohs and their families, on the smooth walls of palaces and temples and in the rolls of papyri.

It was around 3100 that the southern and northern kingdoms were united. It was the south (where the Sumerians would have landed) which conquered the north, possibly with war weapons of bronze (instead of copper), introduced by the Sumerians. Pharaoh Djoser's stepped pyramid, the oldest of them all, appeared at Saqqara, near Memphis, in the north, (c. 2670). Manetho, an Egyptian priest (c.310 BC), compiled an account of the religion and history of his country, basing his information upon the sacred books and the works of the ancient Egyptians. His book includes a list of 30 dynasties of kings from Menes down to the Ptolemaic Period (332-30 BC). In modern times, Egyptian history is conveniently divided into eight periods, after an initial Pre-Dynastic Period (all dates are approximate):

Early Dynastic Period 3100-2686	Second Intermediate Period 1786-1568
Old Kingdom 2686-2181	New Kingdom 1568-1085
First Intermediate Period 2181-2060	Post Empire 1085-333
Middle Kingdom 2060-1786	Ptolemaic 333-30

About 3100, possibly soon after the Sumerians might have appeared in Upper Egypt, the first known ruler of Upper Egypt, Menes (sometimes known as Narmer)

Figure 26. The slate palette of King Narmer (or Menes). From Heirakonopolis, 1st Dynasty c. 3100 BC. On the reverse side (left) the king is wearing the tall White Crown of Upper Egypt, brandishing a mace and killing his foe, perhaps symbolising his conquest of Lower Egypt, in the presence of the falcon god Horus. On the obverse the king is in procession wearing the Red Crown of Lower Egypt. Egyptian Museum, Cairo.

c.2940-2890, conquered Lower Egypt and unified both regions. He is depicted wearing a combined version of the white 'reed leaf' crown of Upper Egypt with that of the red 'bee' crown of Lower Egypt, a diplomatic double crown, with the hieroglyph totemic Falcon denoting the union of the two regions. This Early Dynastic Period (c.3100-2686) witnessed a leap in the social and political development of the kingdom, a huge region, stretching from the Mediterranean a thousand miles down to the First Cataract, and beyond. Narmer's capital was at Memphis. The important geographical isolation of Egypt, placed between the vast, daunting stretches of the Western and the Sinai deserts, gave it immunity from foreign invaders, and invaluable time for its development into a great civilization.

The administrative difficulties of such an immense territory, were greatly facilitated by the course of the Nile, a gigantic chain and a huge highway which tied all governors of the cities along its banks to Pharaoh in Memphis the capital. Inspectors could easily reach any of them in their ships. Shipping was enormously assisted by the prevailing winds from the north, against the strong current of the river; the currents, on the other hand, helped the south-north sailings against the prevailing winds

In a brief essay, an essential aspect of the activities of a people with a long history of over 3000 years, trade might best be given an overall view of its development, rather than be seen as it emerges out of the evolving life of the people as a whole. Shipping was imperative to the survival and growth of Egypt.

From the earliest times, the fertile land along the banks of the Nile yielded essential foodstuff, especially corn and other cereals. A system of canals of increasing complexity watered the more distant arid lands. Other necessary and luxury items were imported from the far south, by boats or rafts down river, or by portage along the river valley. These included copper, arsenic (used for hardening copper into bronze, when tin was not available), incense, oil, gold, ivory, ebony and alabaster.

That trade within the kingdom itself, became increasingly important along the north-south course of the Nile. But certainly, from early times, there was intercourse between the Delta cities and the Sinai with its copper mines and turquoise, as well as with Crete, a short sea crossing to the north. Crete had its own wool to export in exchange for Egyptian goods. In addition, Crete must have offered Egypt many other items which she herself imported via her close trading partners, the Mycenaeans (see chapter 6). The latter obtained rare items such as amber from Scandinavia and tin probably from Bohemia and, among other goods, spices and lapis lazuli from Asia. But, by the third Dynasty (2686-2613) Egypt's own ships were sailing to and from the copper island of Cyprus and the Syrian and Phoenician ports of Ugarit, Byblos, Sidon and Tyre, whence they returned with the goods of the Asiatic hinterlands: timber, bronze, silver, spices, oils, obsidian, lapis lazuli. In payment, the Egyptians exported papyrus, textiles, leather and cereals and later, in the Empire period (from c.1570), items from the south such as ebony and especially gold. They also exported their light chariots.

The Early Dynastic Period, was followed by the Old Kingdom, sometimes called 'the Pyramid Age', (c.2686-2181), a long, prosperous period. Pharaoh Djoser's (c.2686-2613) huge stepped pyramid at Saqqara has been sited above. There must have been many smaller, experimental pyramids, before the construction of that gigantic one became possible. The great stones were cut to the shape of bricks, and were put together like brickwork. Its base is 358 ft from north to south by 410 ft from east to west. The enclosure wall, 33 ft high, is recessed and panelled, which indicates a luxurious, sophisticated social life and organisation. We know the architect's name, Imhotep, who was also a scholar and a philosopher.

Djoser's pyramid was followed by monumental architecture in the Fourth Dynasty (c.2613-2494) of which the three famous pyramids (gigantic pharaonic burial structures) of Cheops (Khufu), Chefren (Khafre) and Mycerinus (Menkaure) at Gaza are the time-defying witnesses. The pyramid of Cheops took 20 years to build (during the flood seasons, each year, when labour was available). It covers 13 acres, representing 760 ft square, more than twice the acreage of St. Peter's, Rome. Originally it was 482 ft high. These massive structures reflect the power and prestige of palace and temple – the kings' unquestioned autocracy and the religious faith of the people in his divinity. The patient, barely rewarded labour (in material terms) of the builders could perhaps be likened to the stonemasons and craftsmen of the European Middle Ages, who devoted their lives to the service of God by expressing their faith in building and embellishing the great cathedrals of which we are the proud heirs.

The famous Sphinx, too, belongs to this era. It is in the form of a recumbent lion with the head of a man, 150 ft long and 65 ft high; the face alone being 13'6" wide and the mouth 8'6". The broken nose dates from Mohammedan times (c.AD 700) and the sculptured beard, which had broken off, is now at the British Museum, London.

These pyramids, temple buildings and artistic activities, as seen today in the form of statues and the usually beautiful graphic art on the walls of palaces, temples and upon royal graves, indicate a stable and rich period in which the hieroglyphic script evolved and the classical language developed. The god-Pharaoh distributed cereals, barley, oil and other goods, stored in the temple warehouses, as wages to the people, after, of course, the priests and nobles had had their ample share. There were, as in all societies, religious rites and celebrations at harvest.

Once the zenith of the period was reached, the inevitable decline set in. By the end of the Old Kingdom (c.2181), and the death of its last king, Peppi II, after a reign of 92 years, Pharaoh's power was challenged by the priests of the sun-god, Re. The rivalry of the numerous nobles and the resulting internecine wars weakened the social structure, accelerating decadence when disciplines weakened and civil servants and administrators forgot old loyalties and moralities. Finally, they could be described as degenerate and corrupt officials, in the midst of a century of civil wars.

Yet, sometimes, it seems to be in such circumstances that literature and the arts flourish greatly (as in the Italian city-states of the High Middle Ages). Not only did the ancient thread of cultural achievements remain unbroken, but during this period, the First Intermediate Period (c.2181-2060), some of Egypt's finest literature appeared – the ancient Egyptian classics.

Life continued to be guided by the cycle of sowing and harvesting, of birth and death. Ordinary people went about their daily tasks as usual. They looked the same. Their dress was minimal: men wore an apron of cotton or leather; women wore a closely-fitting, practically transparent chemise, held by shoulder straps, which, starting below their breasts, reached down to their ankles. The wealthier class had somewhat more elaborate wear.

The position of women appears to have been quite liberal. Monogamy was the general rule, although Pharaoh and those who could afford it had concubines. But an extra legal wife or two for Pharaoh was sometimes necessary for political reasons. Marital relationships seem to have been generally happy, as depicted by the statues of seated pharaohs or noblemen and their spouses, with their arms entwined round each other's waist or shoulders; a tomb-mural (c.2500) shows the wife playing a harp to entertain her reclining husband; it was her prerogative to visit her husband for their conjugal relationship, when she desired to do so. Perhaps the stability of the home promoted the stable government of the Old Kingdom. There were pre-marital relationships, too, – quite romantic ones! A brief example will suffice. It is a poem To Love's Pretence:

> With sickness faint and weary/ All day in bed I'll lie;/ My friends will gather near me/ And she'll with them come nigh./ She'll put to shame the doctors/ Who'll ponder over me,/ For she alone, my loved one,/ Knows well my malady. [1]

There were trial marriages, lasting a year. Then, if not successful, they could be dissolved on payment of a forfeit. Extra-marital relationships were discouraged. Prostitutes and mistresses were ostracised from society. But Pharaohs could marry their own sisters in order to perpetuate their dynasty, as Osiris married his sister Isis.[2]

For, in Egypt the king was god incarnate, unlike the kings of Mesopotamia who were only the representatives of the chief god.

> Pharaoh was not like other men, who became divine after death; he was divine from birth. His father had been the ruling god and his mother the god's wife. On the walls of temples elaborate scenes were carved to remind people of the divine origin of their ruler. At the marriage ceremony, the king impersonated the god, and he was accompanied by his divine attendants. When the king died, the spirit of the god passed to his successor. The son, therefore, according to Egyptian reasoning, became his own father, and, in the theological sense 'husband of his mother'. Horus, who was born after Osiris was slain, was the 'purified image of his sire'. Pharaoh's body was mummified, so that his soul might continue to exist and be able to return to reanimate the bandaged form.[3]

The trinitarian religion of Osiris in which Isis is the mother-wife of Pharaoh, gave Pharaoh his divine status. The cult of Osiris became increasingly popular. It acquired an ethical character. In the scales of justice after death, only those whose good behaviour outweighed their bad deeds would be admitted through the gates of Osiris' paradise. Down to the end of the fourth Dynasty (c.2394), Pharaoh was looked upon as one of the gods, but from the Fifth Dynasty his divinity was deemed as the son of Re (the god of Heliopolis) 'begotten on Pharaoh's human mother, not by a sexual act of his human father, but a non-physical act of the god.'[4, 5, 6]

Mentuhotep II (c.2133-2118) from an aggressive Theban clan, succeeded in re-uniting the land and establishing The Middle Kingdom (c.2133-1786). His achievements are recognised in the title given to him: 'He-Who-Unites-The-Two-Lands'. During this dynasty, the Twelfth (c.1991-1786), a centralised administration revived the traditions of the Old Kingdom. Ministers of State, an army of civil servants, the judges and the police enforced the law; and the somewhat liberated nobility continued to pay their taxes into the royal coffers and supplied contingents in time of war.

The whole population worshipped the god of Thebes, Amun, particularly as he was a successor of, even identified with, the ancient divinity, Re, (hence, 'Amun-Re') who had been placed by the priesthood above a weak Pharaoh. While the immortality of the soul of Pharaoh alone was a royal prerogative in the past, the inestimable hope of happiness in the hereafter it represented was now assured to king and people alike. Their bodies, too, like Pharaoh's could be mummified (if they could afford it), so that it was always available for re-entry of the soul. From the great pyramids down to the mastabas of the rich and the smaller graves of the poor, the necessities of life in the hereafter were buried with the defunct.

Since the new religion broke down class barriers beyond the grave, it also loosened those on earth. Every Egyptian, and even foreigners, had equal rights before the law. The artisan, hitherto tied to a guild or union, was free to follow a trade of his own choice. The ancient power of the guilds had disappeared; trade secrets belonged to the past. Still in the Middle Kingdom, the Twelfth Dynasty shines like a jewel. It heralds the ascent of Egyptian culture and political power. In foreign affairs, colonial Sudan and Nubia in the south became the *entrepôt* for ebony, black slaves and building stone; Ethiopian ivory and gold; myrrh, incense and gum from Punt (Somalia). Copper and turquoise came from Sinai in the north; also from Sinai, the acacia was used for boat building and the sycamore for lighter purposes. There was much business with Crete, Cyprus and Cilicia; ships from Ugarit brought, among other goods, lapis lazuli from Afghanistan, obsidian and heavy building timber from Anatolia and cedar from Lebanon.

Thousands of fresh acres were reclaimed by irrigation, and the resulting wealth promoted trade and public works of all kinds. Of the latter, one of the most amazing is the artificial lake Moeris, still to be seen in the Western Desert, built by order of Pharaoh Amun-emhet III (c.1850). Herodotus (II.149) describes it: 'Its circumference is 3600 stades (c.450 miles), it is 50 fathoms deep. Between the river and the lake he constructed a canal 80 stades (c.10 miles) in length and 300 feet in breadth', through which the waters of the river were admitted or excluded by sluice gates, as required.

That remarkable artificial lake, which must have cost the labour of tens of thousands of men and many years to complete, accommodated the overflow of the river in flood, 'so that it should neither, with its strong current, flood the land unreasonably and form swamps and fens, nor, by rising less than was advantageous, damage the crops by lack of water.' (Herod II, 49) The great lake, built nearly 4000 years ago, still remains and functions as it was intended, to serve the peasant-farmers of the Fayum oasis, whose existence depends upon its waters.

Literature of the period in prose and verse achieved classical perfection and the religious poems are equal to the greatest and most profound of Oriental literature. Art, although not evoking the solid perpetuity of that of the Old Kingdom, reached a delicacy and sensitivity comparable to the best of earlier achievements, especially in sculpture.

The Middle Kingdom came to a sudden, mysterious end. The principle of rise, zenith and decline, seems to apply here, as it does in everything else. It is a time of change – The Second Intermediate Period (c.2010-1786). The country fell into a state of anarchy. This, the eighteenth century BC, coincides with the brilliant reign of Babylon's King Hammurabi (1793-1750).

It was at the end of this period also that an army composed of refugees, nomads and a variety of hangers-on – Semites, Aryans (who were appearing at this time from the north and the east), Canaanites – a motley crowd described as the Hyksos or 'rulers of foreign lands', more popularly recognised as 'the Shepherd Kings', crossed the Sinai Desert, infiltrated and finally seized the Delta region, which they ruled for one hundred and fifty years (c.2010-1786) from their new capital, Avaris. The true Pharaohs were relegated to Upper Egypt, ruling their remaining territory in the south from Thebes. There were other peoples in the

Delta region, foreigners like the Hyksos themselves, who had settled down and were prepared to cooperate with their new masters. It was the Hyksos Pharaoh Apophis (c.1630) who would have protected the Hebrew Joseph (and his tribe), if, as suggested (see chapter 4), the Jews had entered Egypt together with the Hyksos.

Before that invasion, the pharaohs and their people had had an inbred sense of security. Since the beginning, the only 'enemies' were the inferior Nubians and other unsophisticated peoples who, far from constituting a threat to Egyptian security, were used as slaves or exploited for mining and 'advantageous' barter. The Western and the Sinai deserts were the almost impenetrable bastions and barriers against any predators. The Hyksos disaster demonstrated that the world outside had been transformed and that the ancient foreign policy, leadership and organisation of the armed forces must be adapted to meet the new military and political changes.

A resurgent Dynasty, the eighteenth, using weapons and tactics of war perhaps adopted from the Hyksos themselves, expelled the invaders, after a war of 45 years and a three-year siege of the Hyksos capital, Avaris. The royal house of Egypt was re-established over the whole of Egypt and the glorious New Kingdom (c. 1567-1085) was born – the apogee of Egyptian civilization and the dawn of the Egyptian Empire in Asia. The Eighteenth Dynasty (c.1567-1320), was perhaps the most brilliant in Egyptian history. It produced Pharaoh Amosis I (c.1570-1549), who reorganised the country, tightened the social structure, forged a new army with regiments of splendid light, horse-drawn chariots (as depicted on wall paintings in temples and palaces) and bronze weapons. He expelled the Hyksos and pursued them across the Sinai, and invaded their homelands in southern Palestine and Asia. But Joseph's descendants, the Jews, who, as suggested above, had settled in Egypt with the Hyksos, were left behind as slaves and servants of Egyptian masters (see chapter 4). Tuthmoses I (c.1525-1512) continued the military triumphs of Amosis and his successors. We see him in Palestine, Jordan and northern Syria and, later, far to the east, in the Euphrates region where kingdoms and principalities submitted to Pharaoh. He established garrisons and native governors to collect tribute for Egypt.

The energetic Pharaohs of the enriched land of the Nile, could once more afford to demonstrate their allegiance to the gods (and the powerful priesthood) by repairing old temples and building new ones at Thebes, which became the religious centre for the worship of the chief god, Amun. Its many statues, carvings and paintings together represent fascinating historical documents.

The two children of Tuthmoses I, Tuthmoses II and Hatshepsut, were married to one another. They ascended the throne as king and queen after the death of their father. But Hatsheptsut's brother-husband died after only eight years and would have been succeeded by Tuthmoses III, a son by Tuthmoses I's concubine, had he been allowed to do so by the powerful palace faction which supported Hatshepsut. In any case, he was only a child, so Hatshepsut acted as regent. She was the 'Queen Elizabeth' of Egypt, who patronised the arts. The walls of her magnificent temple at Deir el Bahri are covered with richly conceived paintings. The temple gleams like a jewel carved out of the mountain side. She re-established the failing religious rites and with the support of a grateful priesthood and her courtiers, ruled well for sixteen years, encouraging trading relationships everywhere, especially with the land of Punt (perhaps modern Somalia) for its incense trees and other luxuries.

When at last she died, Tuthmoses III (1504-1450) who had been a nominal joint ruler, took over the reins of government. He is considered to be the greatest of the warrior pharaohs – the Alexander – of Ancient Egypt. During his sixteen years in historical limbo, under Hatshepsut's regency and usurpation, he associated himself closely with the army, which he reorganised. It was no longer fragmented, each part under its respective lord, but a single unit under his own direct command. He also inherited the new, revolutionary instrument of war, the two-wheeled, light chariot, drawn by galloping horses, trained for battle.

The enemy, the 'hated Asiatics', was beyond the Sinai desert. Firstly the 'vile' one, the King of Kadesh, in the Lebanon, had to be subdued; then the Aryan kingdoms of Mitanni and subsequently the 'abominable Kheta', the Hittites (see chapter 7, *Anatolia*). The latter had already, in 1595, swept down the Euphrates and in a surprise attack, sacked Babylon and plundered its rich temples. Tuthmoses III led his army out of Sinai and after a march of ten days, appeared before Gaza. He seized it for a base whence he could operate against Megiddo, the key city of the 'vile Asiatics', which would open the gates for Egypt's northern campaigns. The strategically situated Megiddo was at the northern end of the valley between two ranges of mountains overlooking the Plains of Syria, leading to the capital, Kadesh on the upper Orontes, near the south bank of Lake Homs. The king held a Council of War with his officers. The shortest route was through the valley, but it was so narrow that chariots and soldiers would have to cross it in single file. The enemy could slaughter them to a man. The king's officers suggested two alternative, less dangerous, though longer routes which would bring them out on the north side of Megiddo. The high spirited, young king declared that he for one and his charioteer would charge through the valley, a foolhardy but quite unexpected enterprise which would take the enemy completely by surprise. He probably had had information from his secret agents denied to others. He told the despondent officers:

> Let him of you who wishes go upon those roads you speak of, and let him of you who wishes come to the train of My Majesty. Do not let these enemies whom (the god) Re abominates say 'Has His Majesty proceeded along another road because he has grown afraid of us?' For that is what they will say.[7]

The officers reply that 'we are in the train of Thy Majesty wherever Thy Majesty will go. The servant will follow the master'.[8] So, at the appointed time, they and their troopers followed their king, pelting through the valley. It was only when the main body was safely through that the astonished King of Kadesh, stationed near Megiddo, realised how the Egyptians had successfully taken advantage of his carelessness. It was late afternoon. Both sides prepared for battle the following day. In the morning the enemy was faced by the Egyptian cavalry and troops rank upon rank, the armoured king upon his chariot of gleaming electrum. In despair they had recourse to a stratagem, probably Mitannian: they released a mare into the ranks of the enemy chariots. But before she could disrupt the high spirited stallions, a king's officer records how he 'pursued after her on foot, and with my sword I ripped open her belly; I cut off her tail, I set it before the king . . .'[9] The enemy was routed. They abandoned everything, including their waggons of treasure and sought shelter in Megiddo. Tuthmoses besieged that city and took it. His triumph was complete at that great battle of Megiddo (1479). It established the Egyptian Empire in Asia. The campaigns yielded enormous loot and slaves, and the opulent cosmopolitan society which followed, produced a golden age of architecture and painting at Luxor, Karnak and Abu Simbel. Much of the temple building reflected the power of the priesthood of Amun, whose chief religious centre was Pharaoh's capital, Thebes.

The glory of Egypt came to its apogee under Amun-hotep III (1417-1379) and his much younger queen, Tiy, who is said to have exercised considerable influence in shaping Egypt's domestic and foreign policies. Under pressure of old age, he abdicated in favour of his idealistic and monotheistic son, Amun-hotep IV (1379-1362), better known as Akhenaten, after Aten, the Sun, Akhenaten's only god. He rebelled against the powerful Amun priests, openly adopted the monotheistic worship of Aten, and moved with his wife, the celebrated beauty, Nefertiti, and his court to a new city called, after his god, Akhet-Aten, on the site of today's Tell el Amarna. Then, the ancient god Amun's effigies, temples and monuments were destroyed, his name was eradicated wherever it appeared and replaced by that of Aten, and the word for 'gods' was changed to the singular, 'god'.[10] Akhenaten's parents witnessed this revolutionary change of the religious and secular centre from Thebes to Akhetaten (henceforth Amarna). That new and shining city claimed much of the priestly income from the worshippers of Amun which weakened the disproportionate power of the priesthood. Thus did Akhenaten earn the dangerous priestly hatred.

The taxes they had extracted from Amun's adherents were now imposed upon them by the priests and temples of Aten but especially by the new liberal government of Akhenaten at Amarna. He and his queen, Nefertiti, were now able to express their idealism by throwing open the gates of their new city and inviting craftsmen, artists, architects and philosophers and those of the population who embraced the new and more reasonable religion to make Amarna their home. There was a new spirit of liberty which expressed itself in new forms of art and thought. The ancient stiff-limbed portraiture and formal stance of figures in art were replaced by natural movements expressing love or other emotions. Original literature, that of poetry and philosophy, was permanently recorded on papyrus or tablets by the busy scribes, in hieroglyphics. These we can read after over 3000 years.

When, after a glorious reign, the aged Amunhotep III died, the elaborate funeral ceremonies were performed in the temple of Amun at Thebes; his body was mummified or embalmed. Mummification offered incomparable opportunities for the furtherance of the study of anatomy and medicine. The process was, of course, carried out by the priests who were consequently also the learned physicians of Egypt. Traditionally, religion and magic were introduced into the complicated scientific exercise of removing the viscera and pulling out the brain through the nostrils by fine hooked wires and placing all the parts in four tightly sealed canopic jars as part of the material in the defunct's tomb. The body was then covered in raw pitch or resin and dried, wrapped in unimaginable lengths of linen bandages and placed in a richly decorated coffin made of the rarest wood. After a period of seventy days, it was interred, to rest with his ancestors. Mummifying the dead body, be it that of royalty or nobleman and even certain sacred animals, especially Anubis (the black jackal-god who guarded the tomb), enhanced and perpetuated the power of the priests. For those who could not afford costly processes, more inferior materials were used or, if very poor, they were buried in the hot, sterile sands of the desert where the body survived beyond the lifetime of relatives.

Who was the mysterious Nefertiti of aristocratic beauty? She had grown up as the playmate of Akhenaten, heir to the throne, a shy and thoughtful boy. Her origin is unknown but that she was fair (and even probably blue-eyed) is not disputed. Both children were tutored by the wise and highly respected scholar, loyal philosopher and astute vizier-diplomat, Ay, comparable to the builder of Djoser's Pyramid, Imhotep. It is said that Nefertiti might have been Ay's daughter by one of the many Mitannian concubines sent to Pharaoh Amunhotep III by Tushratta, king of Mitanni, with many other gifts in exchange for the abundant Egyptian gold (the Mitannians were an Aryan ruling class over a Hurrian people (see chapter 7)). The two young people grew up as brother and sister and were duly married. After marriage, the happy couple, strong adherents to the worship of Aten, the one and only god (the golden Sun and its beneficent rays) removed their capital, royal city from Amun's Thebes to Aten's Akhet-Aten (Amarna), where all thought of foreign and home affairs, ultimately the responsibility of Pharaoh, were forgotten in continuing to build an ideal and beautiful city and in entertaining and being enertained by artists and philosophers.

In AD 1887 a peasant woman, while digging for fertiliser on the site of Pharaoh Akhenaten's capital, now the archaeological site of El Amarna, came upon more than 3000 tablets with cuneiform script (now known as the 'Amarna Tablets' or 'Amarna Letters'). They proved to be the diplomatic correspondence (c.1400 BC) mainly in Akkadian, between Egypt's Amunhotep III and Akhenaten on the one side, and the kings of Hatti, Mitanni, Babylonia and the Egyptian colonial governors of various cities in Syria and Palestine on the other. The internationalism, the *lingua franca*, of Akkadian, is well illustrated by the Akkadian-scripted tablets, addressed to Ugarit in Syria, where a distinct Semitic language was spoken, and a particular alphabetic system of cuneiform writing had been invented (this being employed above all for the native Canaanite literature). The Akkadian language was used to a considerable extent for official and legal purposes. Sumerian remained the language of scholars and temple priests.

Among the Amarna correspondence of the two kings, Amunhotep III and his son, Akhenaten, with foreign potentates, there are also appeals for help from Akhenaten's own hard pressed generals and governors in Asia, all of which appear to have been ignored by Pharaoh. One example from the last governor of the great and wealthy seaport of Byblos will suffice to illustrate the apparent perversity of Akhenaten. He begs the king to let him
march against him and smite him (the enemy) . . . . The land is the King's

land, and since I have talked thus you have not moved the city has been lost. There is no money to buy horses, all is finished, we have been sopiled. . . give me thirty companies of horse with chariot, men, men . . . there is none of this for me . . . not a horse. [11]

Akhenaten's idealism or indolence (he is sometimes called the first pacifist) finally caused the loss of Egypt's empire in Asia and brought about social chaos at home. On his death the Amun priests tried to destroy every vestige of the hated Pharaoh and his beautiful queen, as well as the temples and name of his god Aten. In modern times, a bust of Nefertiti was found by German archaeologists in a dustbin at Amarna. It is now exhibited at the Berlin Museum. The god Amun was reinstated and the holy capital city of Thebes re-established.

Two young boys succeeded one another to the throne, the last one being the famous Tutankh-Aten, perhaps a son of Akhenaten's by one of his daughters (since Nefertiti had already produced six daughters and no sons). His name was changed by the Amun priests to Tutankhamun. He ascended the throne at the age of nine and with his 13-year-old queen was taken with great pomp to Thebes where he was crowned in the great temple of Amun which, together with all other Amun temples and statuary were being rebuilt or refurbished. However, Tutankhamun, like his brother, died in his late 'teens'. In the absence of a successor in the direct line of the XVIIIth dynasty, Tutankh-Amun's young widow, Ankhesen-Amun (or, as some authorities believe, Nefertiti herself) horrified to find that, in the absence of a more eligible partner, she would have to marry either her aged tutor, Ay, or, worse, perhaps the old commander-in-chief, Horemheb, of humble background, begged Egypt's traditional enemy, king Shuppiluliumas of the 'abominable Kheta' (the Hittites), to send her his son and she would marry him. This could have been a major disaster for Egypt, for then it might have become part of the Hittite empire. On the other hand, the young queen's adviser, probably, Ay, might have envisaged the acquisition by Egypt of a prince from the powerful Hittite royal house, backed by the vigour of its people, to support and revivify Egypt. Queen Ankhesen-Amun wrote to king Shuppiluliumas:

My husband has died, and I have no son. They say about you that you have many sons. You might give me one of your sons, and he might become my husband. I would not want to take one of my servants. I am loath to make him my husband.

The Hittite king was amazed at such a message from a queen of the formidable, ancient Egyptian empire. He sent his chamberlain to verify the queen's sincerity. Indignantly she wrote again:

Why do you doubt me? If I had a son, would I write a letter which humiliates me and my people? I have no sons. Am I to take a humble servant for my husband?[7]

Shuppiluliumas was persuaded to send one of his sons, with a bridal party.

Horemheb, the scorned 'servant', having been informed of the plot which would deny him the Egyptian throne, sent 'Egyptians with many horses . . . the prince was captured and poisoned'[12] near the Egyptian frontier. Ay, now aged, well over 80, pilot of the policies of three kings (Amunhotep III, Akhenaten and

Tutankhamun), and himself distantly related to the dynasty, ascended the throne, taking care to keep the goodwill of the commander-in-chief of the armed forces, Horemheb, close to him. Ay then reigned for perhaps two years, and died c.1342, perhaps poisoned by Horemheb at the same time as the unfortunate queen Ankhesen-Amun. The ambitious and villainous Horemheb, who had the support of the army, then married Akhenaten's sister and thus made himself eligible for the golden throne of Egypt. He was the last, and least respected, of the brilliant XVIIIth Dynasty Pharaohs, in spite of the fact that he secured the frontiers of Egypt and brought a semblance of order to the state. He ordered the thorough destruction, indeed the annihilation, of the beautiful city of Amarna, with all its treasures, works of art and architecture.

The long list of the great, native Egyptian warrior Pharoahs closes with Rameses II (1290-1224) of the XIXth Dynasty. Many of the gigantic, dramatic monuments of Egypt are his. It was he who fought the last battle with the Hittites and their many allies, including the Mitanni (see chapter 7 *Anatolia*), at Kadesh on the river Orontes. Rameses had impetuously ridden, in his magnificent, light chariot, covered with electrum (alloy of gold and silver), accompanied by his bodyguard of equally enthusiastic young men, through the same narrow valley traversed by Tuthmoses III, leaving the main army doing its best to keep up. He and his companions emerged from the valley to find themselves surrounded by the enemy, the Hittites. Rameses and his companions put up a great, valiant fight until the main body of the Egyptian army came to their rescue and the battle was 'won' after two-days' hard fighting. [13]

In documents found respectively at Thebes and Hattusa (Boghaz Köy), the Hittite capital, both sides claim to have been the victors. It was probably a 'draw', and they withdrew to their respective frontiers. In his long reign Rameses fought other battles with the Hittites, until, in the face of the rising might of Assyria (King Shalmaneser I 1275-42), the traditional enemies signed a treaty of peace, respect for each other's boundaries and mutual assistance against every danger: a diplomatic pact (1269), said to be the first of its kind, which still exists in two languages. Rameses married the Hittite king's (Hattusilis III 1289-65) daughter, and the Hittite king himself travelled to Egypt in great pomp to attend the wedding.

The reign of Rameses III (1182-1151) of the XXth Dynasty, falls within a period of great movements of peoples, in eastern Europe and western Asia. The period could be described as an historical watershed (see chapter 8 *The Sea Peoples*). Some of these peoples headed for Egypt and the former Egyptian colonies along the Syria-Palestine coast. Fortunately, Rameses III proved himself to be a worthy leader at that critical time. His wars against the invasions of 'the Sea Peoples', particularly the (Biblical) Philistines, probably known as the Paleset, were successful. Rameses describes his preparations against the threat of invasion:

> I prepared the river-mouth like a strong wall with warships, galleys and light craft. They were completely equipped both fore and aft with brave fighters carrying weapons, and infantry of all the pick of Egypt, being like roaring lions on the mountains; chariotry with able warriors and goodly officers whose hands were competent. [14]

The battle was won and the Sea Peoples were driven away. The surviving

Philistines settled along the coast of Palestine. East of their territory were the Israelites who, under the leadership of Joshua, had taken advantage of the chaotic political situation in the region, successfully attacked Jericho and established the historical Jewish kingdom (c.1180, Josh. VI.20,14).

The wars against the Philistines (and others) were fought and won by ancient Egypt, under the last of their *great* Pharaohs:

> It was 2,000 years since Hor-Aha united the Two Lands. It was 400 years since Ahmose (or Amosis) began to drive out the Hyksos. It was more than three centuries since Tuthmoses III won the battle of Megiddo and 111 years after the Battle of Kadesh. As Rameses III sailed triumphantly up-river to Thebes and heard the rising murmur of the crowds lining the banks; as the golden barges of the god Amun came out to meet him from the Quays of Karnak, was he aware of the conquerors who had served Egypt centuries before he was born? Did he hear, above the clamour, the roar of Menkheperre's (Thutmoses III) charioteers at Megiddo, or the high, clear scream of the trumpets before Kadesh?[15]

Henceforth, it is a slow decline. The Dynastic Tables come to an end one thousand years later when Egypt becomes a Roman colony. After Rameses III, it is only in the Old Testament that the petty pharaohs are remembered with dread, as, for example, Shishak (c. 930), a very insignificant pharaoh, who captured Jerusalem, and carried away the treasures of Solomon's temple.

Notes

1. Mackenzie Donald, *Egyptian Myths & Legends*, London, 1913, p. 61

2. Frazer James, *The Golden Bough*, London 1941, p. 363

3. Mackenzie Donald, ibid, pp. 105-6.

4. *Ibid*, p. xxxvi;

5. Frazer James, *The Golden Bough*, op. cit., p. 383

6. Toynbee Arnold, Mankind and Mother Earth, Oxford University Press, 1976, pp. 74, 289-90.

7. Breasted J.H., *Ancient Records of Egypt, vol. 2*, Chicago University Press, 1906; quoted by Leonard Cottrell, *The Warrior Pharaohs*, Evans Bros, London, 1968.

8. Breasted J.H., ibid.

9. Breasted J.H., ibid.

10. Aldred Cyril, *The Armana Period and the End of the 18th Dynasty*, CAH II², p. 18.

11. Erman A. and Blackman, *Literature of Ancient Egypt*, Methuen 1927, quoted by Leonard Cottrell, *The Warrior Pharaohs*, London, 1968.

12. Desroches-Nobelcourt Christian, *Tutankhamun*, Michael Joseph, London, 1969.

13. Gardiner A.H., *Egypt of the Pharaohs*, Clarendon Press, Oxford, 1961.

14. Breasted J.H., ibid.

15. Gardiner A.H., *Egypt of the Pharaohs*, op.cit.

Chapter 6
Crete and Mycenae

Although Crete is in Europe and might therefore seem to be irrelevant to a history of the Near East, its importance as a link between Sumer-Babylon, Egypt and Greece in Europe, should be described, at least very briefly, because Greek civilization was born much later from the aggregate womb of those ancient cultures of the Near East, including Crete.

Sir Arthur Evans, while in Athens in 1893, came upon small, triangular and square stones, with symbols which seemed to belong to a hieroglyphic system. They were in dealers' shops and in the collection of Heinrich Schliemann, who had discovered what were believed to be the ancient sites of Troy and Mycenae. Evans was informed that the inscribed stones had been found in Crete. He had already considered Crete as a stepping stone for the route of hieroglyphic writing from Egypt to Greece. In 1899 he began excavations on the site of Knossos, where in his search for clues to decipher the system of writing engraved on his mysterious seals, he stumbled upon the remains of a great and very ancient civilization. It was extensively excavated under his supervision, many of the fallen pieces were replaced in their original positions and the beautiful and unique palace buildings and decorations were largely restored at his own expense. Excavations and the study of material they revealed continued after his death in 1941.

During the Neolithic period (c.6000), Crete had very little, if any, contact with the outside world. It is poor in minerals; but by 2500-2300, through contact perhaps initially with Egypt, then with the Cycladic islands, Cyprus and the Syria-Palestine ports, Crete had learnt the techniques of applying copper and bronze, gold and silver and stone to highly original practical, artistic and aesthetic ends.

The culture of Crete is called the Minoan, after the legendary king Minos, and Cretans are often referred to as Minoans. The Middle Minoan, the Golden Age of Minoan civilization, flourished between 2000-1650. Crete, with its unwalled cities, was respected as a great naval and political power in Asia and Egypt as well as on mainland Greece. It had important trading relations with Mycenae and other centres in the Peloponnese. All this brought wealth to Crete, making possible great palace complexes, decorated with frescoes which take one into a world of fantasy and artistry of the first order.

Evans saw similarities between Libyan tholoi (beehive-shaped stone tombs) and those of the Messara region on the south coast of Crete; Egyptian funerary-type figurines and certain stone bowls discovered in Crete, are evidence of contact with Egypt, probably during the high era of the Egyptian Old Kingdom from the Fourth to the Sixth Dynasties (2613-2181).[1] Also, significantly, Cretan man's waist cloth or skirt is noticeably African in style.[2] There seems to have been an irregular connection between the Egyptians of the Delta and early Crete.

On the mainland of Greece, between c.2300 and c.1800, when Crete was a flourishing civilization, material remains are so poor that we are astonished at the illustrious period of high culture that followed, albeit a thousand years later. Cretan objects, 18th and 17th century cups and vases, found in graves among native pottery of that period at Athens, stand witness to infiltration of Cretan influence:

> The gold cups of Vaphio, with their repoussé designs of bull hunting, represent the high water mark of Minoan art – for Minoan they are, whether the artist worked in Crete or Laconia . . . from fragmentary remains at Mycenae and elsewhere, we can deduce that many Minoan factories were early adapted: more finely cut masonry, the decorative carving in stone, and a full use of fresco painting on walls, in style virtually indistinguishable from the Minoan.[3]

Traders from Asia Minor and Syria-Palestine came to the Greek mainland via the Cycladic islands, before the Cretans. All the islands had harbours for the small Bronze Age (c. 3000-1200) vessels. An important, extensive seafaring trade also developed between the peoples of Asia and Crete.

But superior post-2500 Cretan-style articles appear in Asia far more extensively than Asiatic articles in Crete. Thus, the teachers seem to have been overtaken by their pupils.

Minoan hieroglyphic picture writing, original in style but similar to Egyptian, appears to have given way from a pictographic to a more sophisticated script, the Minoan 'Linear A' (c.1750-c.1450), still largely undeciphered. It represents the key to the original, still unknown language, used throughout Crete during the eighteenth and fifteenth centuries.[4] However, the Mycenaean merchant-traders seem to have adapted the 'Linear A' script to their own language (c. 1450 - c. 1400), which was not necessarily Greek. That version is known as 'Linear B', a syllabic script. Unlike 'A', 'B' was found only in Knossos, the Minoan-Mycenaean trading centre, and in no other part of Crete. 'B' was also indistinguishable from the examples found on mainland Greece, the home of the Mycenaeans. It consists chiefly of proper names and inventories, which could be in a language other than Greek.

In 1951, Michael Ventris deciphered the Mycenaean 'Linear B'. In his highly respected opinion, it was Greek. It included pictograms of chariots, amphora, and horses. Evans had guessed that the signs represented an inventory. Hence, the language of 'Linear A' was that of a people, the native Cretans themselves, who created the Minoan Golden Age; the script was originally invented for that still unknown language. It was later adapted by the Mycenaeans to their own language in the form known as 'Linear B'.

As in Babylonia, so in Crete, writing was essential for the proper administration of extensive territories and for recording large quantities of a variety of goods. The advantages of writing came to Crete after 2000, over a thousand years after Sumer. By 2000, the Aegean was still far behind Mesopotamia in most aspects of civilization, and much of the culture it possessed must have been founded on that of Sumer-Akkad, via the great city-state sea-ports such as Ugarit and Byblos.

In Crete there is not a single tablet, not a single word, which describes 'buying' or 'selling' of goods. But there is a large quantity of tablets listing stocks of goods and names. Minoan society must therefore have been directed by the king's seneschals, responsible for the distribution of the wealth and the internal economy in every detail. No money in any form was involved. Payment in kind was made for services, and in the export trade, wool from great flocks of Cretan sheep and, later on, textiles, wine and oil, as well as timber, were exchanged for imports of copper, tin, gold, ivory, faience (decorated fine earthenware and transparent glaze (porcelain)) and precious stones (especially for their seals), the raw materials for which were not to be found in Crete.[5]

Minoan merchants (*Keftiu*) are portrayed on Egyptian frescoes, carrying folded (woollen) cloths. But they are also seen carrying gold, silver, ivory and other objects, which might represent Egyptian payment for Minoan exports to Egypt. Crete, then, was manifestly a wealthy commercial and maritime empire, as witnessed by the magnificent, luxurious palaces at Knossos, and its experienced seamen, who made the administration of such an empire possible.

At this stage, c.1650, Minoan civilization appears to have been at its zenith, when the first catastrophic explosion of the volcanic island of Thera (Santorin), about 110 km. north of Crete, took place. The magnitude of that explosion has been a matter of controversy. An article by John Crossland in the *Observer* newspaper of Sunday 26th November 1989, describes 'the startling theory of Dr Michael Baillie of Queen's University, Belfast,' as to the colossal eruption and dating of the explosion, which was 'several times more powerful than that of Krakatoa,' (in AD 1833 which caused world-wide disturbances). Dr. Baillie's theory as to the date and intensity of the first explosion of Thera, is based on the bog oaks (preserved over periods of millennia) which

> had very narrow rings for the decade of the 1620's BC. Comparing them with sulphuric acid deposits left by eruptions on the Greenland ice sheet, he concluded that there had been a natural disaster caused by Thera which affected the entire northern hemisphere. It threw four cubic miles of material into the atmosphere, covering the nearby Minoan civilization on Crete with ash and tidal waves. In addition, thick cloud may have blotted out the sun for months, if not years, bringing about a massive climatic change. Dr Bailie's work and research by other archaeologists suggests the Minoans survived the explosion, then succumbed to the poorer environment left in its wake.

That horrendous disaster, however, destroyed mainly the eastern part of the island. Knossos in the north-west and probably also Phaistos in the south survived and remained powerful city-states for another two centuries. References are made by classical Greek writers to the Minoan maritime empire or thalassocracy. Although the Mycenaean kings, (perhaps descendants of Anatolian invaders who overran the Greek mainland, c. 2100) were for a time, possibly, tributaries to Crete,[6] it is difficult to establish the existence of a military-based Minoan empire. In Crete itself, there are no signs of any military equipment, chariots or spears, shields or helmets, fortresses or walled cities, before the invasion of the Mycenaeans,

Figure 27. The Prince with the Lilies. Fresco from Heraclion Museum, Knossos.

following the second explosion of Santorin (c.1450, see below). This situation is unique to Crete. Such a palace-centred social organisation resembles Ugarit, Byblos or Mari, but without their military hardware or their protective city walls. It is only after the Mycenaean invasion in the fifteenth century BC that military equipment, buried in warrior shaft-graves, is to be found.

Yet the story of Athenian subjection to Crete, during the Bronze Age, and of the hero, Theseus, who perhaps symbolises rebellion (c.1450) against the Minoan king Minos, belies the appearance of peaceful relationships everywhere. King Minos demands an annual sacrifice of Athenian youths and maidens to the monster-god, half man half bull, the Minotaur, which resides in the centre of a labyrinth at Knossos. Theseus, one of the youths included in the annual consignment of victims, is guided by Ariadne, daughter of Minos, through the labyrinth, to the Minotaur, which he slays. The pair then flee to the island of Naxos, where Theseus deserts Ariadne. The god, Dionysus, finds and marries her.

Bronze statuettes of bulls in cult centres, usually caves, suggest that the bull was an important element in Minoan religion, as a sacrificial or ritualistic animal. The Minotaur legend, of which the central theme is sacrifice to a bull, might have been an attempt to explain initiation ceremonies involved in the worship of Dionysus. Although the bull was an important symbol in Minoan religion, and ritualistic sacrifices were indeed made to it, it is difficult to give the Theseus legend credence, symbolising Athenian subjection to Crete. Subject peoples who overthrow their masters and regain their independence, do not wrap up such heroic achievements in the folds of obscure legends. On the contrary they are very specific about (and often exaggerate) the valiant manner in which independence was gained.

The possible date of the Athenian Theseus' exploit (c.1450) coincides approximately with the tragic devastation of Crete – worst in the eastern regions – caused by the second explosion of the volcanic Santorin-Thera. The legend might well symbolise that historically documented event. Did the Athenians invest themselves with the Mycenaean rebellion? For it was probably during that time of Cretan distress and weakness, that the Mycenaeans seized the opportunity to throw off Cretan supremacy and invaded Crete by assuming military guise instead of that of merchants.

Cretan kings differed widely from any of the early rulers of Asia, who filled their cities with monumental buildings and statues of god-kings to emphasise their own power, which was harnessed to those of their gods. Minoan rulers appear to have been much more modest in the display of their wealth, much more 'democratic' in their hidden, dictatorial powers. The numerous Minoan gods were adored in the home or in caves rather than in large, fearsome temples. The typical public expression of worship was ritual dancing.

The religious symbolic objects were the double-axe (*labrys*) and the 'horns of consecration', and there is evidence of sacrifices, sheep, pigs and dogs, besides bulls. Objects dedicated to the gods included a distinctive pottery and a variety of feminine articles, animal statuettes and eventually, human figurines, including the well-known 'Snake-goddess' which was probably an oriental idea. These articles seem to indicate a tradition of 'smallness' of scale.

Large frescoes are uncommon and seldom represent human figures. Minoan art has an original delicacy and technical skill in creating small, beautiful articles, rarely found in the Bronze Age (c. 3000-1200). Vases, for example, made from a variety of material, including the native gypsum which can easily be polished to an exceptional brightness, decorated with attractive designs of sea creatures, reached a zenith of originality. Remains of a diorite statue of a seated man, with Egyptian hieroglyphics around its base, were found by Evans near the Knossos throne room, a solid witness to Egyptian 'presence' in Cretan affairs. In visual arts, Minoan society demonstrated its highly sophisticated life-style, unlike any other in antiquity.

They appear to be a 'beautiful' people, with few serious concerns: deep passion, sorrow or joy are not evident. They are familiar with the basic modern luxuries of fashion, physical comforts, good drainage and ventilation; they enjoy the circus and the national quasi-ritualistic sport or gymnastics of great skill, with their sacred bulls, which they do not harm within the precincts of the theatre. In short, many aspects of their activities portray them as a civilized people, in the best sense of the expression.

This statement is supported by the liberal social status of their women. They seem to have had an important role in all aspects of the community – not only in social life but certainly in religious matters and most likely in government of the state, too. They appear to be on an equal footing with men, as depicted on the frescoes at Knossos in social scenes at Court, comparable to similar situations in our own times.

> In some frescoes, we see the ladies of Minos' court depicted sitting at the windows of the palace, openly and unveiled. Their dress is extraordinarily modern in appearance: it is *décolleté*, with bare necks and arms, the breasts covered apparently with gold or silver guards reproducing their outline, their waists pinched in and, below, ample skirts with parallel rows of flounces, resembling nothing so much as the *crinolines* of the mid- nineteenth century.[7]

This describes the fashionable Late Minoan ladies of Knossos. Their coiffure 'with its knots and side-curls, closely resembles that of the ladies of the Court of Charles II.'[8]

The dress of the men consisted merely of a waist-cloth over which was worn a short kilt. As opposed to the simple Egyptian white waist cloth, the Minoan equivalent

> was ornamented in the usual way with spiral and other designs in bright colour . . . the upper part of the men's body was nude but for a necklace, except when, on occasions of ceremony, and doubtless often by older men, a gala robe was donned.[9] [In short], Knossos seems to be eloquent of the teeming life and energy of a young and beauty-loving people for the first time feeling its creative power and exulting with the pure *joie de vivre* . . . . No inhuman Egyptian Pharaoh received here the worship due to a god from prostrate ministers and retainers. The halls of Knossos were inhabited by a crowd of courtiers, men and women both, who surrounded the king, and lived with him to enjoy the good things of life.

The second great volcanic outburst of Santorin (c. 1450) destroyed that life-style for ever, for it was followed by the invasion of a relatively savage people – the Mycenaeans.

> The blast from the explosion would have wrecked the settlements along the coast and far inland. The ash rising from the crater must have enveloped the whole of Crete in total darkness for days on end. Earthquakes may have accompanied the eruption, but this is uncertain. Lamps and fires were evidently lit in the shattered settlements, and as houses collapsed in ruins, they started conflagrations of which the traces are evident on many of the wrecked sites such as Zakro and Knossos. With the collapse of the great subterranean void left by the explosion, huge tidal waves (*tsunamis*) were formed and swept down upon the coasts of Crete, causing further havoc, while poisonous vapours from the volcano spread sickness among the survivors. Worse was to follow: the wind, blowing from the north-west at the time, spread a layer of volcanic debris at least 10 centimetres thick, it has been estimated, over the whole of the eastern part of Crete. Nothing would grow; the surviving population must have had to leave their homes or starve. For several decades the eastern part of the island would have been a desert. This abandonment of East Crete is reflected in the absence of any pottery there dating from the Late Minoan II period (1450-1400) which falls between the time of the catastrophe in Late Minoan IB (c. 1450) and the beginning of Late Minoan IIIA (c. 1425).

> This catastrophe must have made the deepest impression on the whole civilized world at the time. The cloud of darkness would have reached as far as Egypt, while the *tsunamis* swept the coasts of Syria-Palestine and the Delta area. It was perhaps by taking advantage of the darkness and confusion that the children of Israel escaped from bondage in Egypt. The book of Exodus describes how the 'darkness over the land of Egypt, even darkness which may be felt' lasted three days; and this may be no exaggeration.[10]

The Mycenaean kings were for a time, perhaps, tributaries to Crete, but after the second catastrophe they seem to have taken advantage of the general confusion and established themselves as masters of Crete, adding that historic island to their own quasi-independent tributaries, such as the Cyclades and possibly Rhodes and Miletus (Millawanda) on the Ionian coast all of which might be described as their loosely-knit maritime empire. It is from this time (after 1450) that military hardware – shields, helmets, chariots – and warrior shaft graves are to be found on Cretan soil. Henceforth the Minoans themselves seem to experience intermittent rise and fall in their cultural experience, as the flicker of a candle before it finally expires.

The most persuasive proof of Mycenaean colonisation of Crete is the controversial statement by a school of archaeologist-historians that the Mycenaean language of 'Linear B' tablets found at Knossos is not (as already suggested) necessarily Greek. It consists mainly of short inscriptions, on clay tablets, mostly bureaucratic lists of proper names, which need not be Greek. There are ten times as many 'Linear B' tablets, all found at Knossos (which most scholars accept, was the centre of Mycenaean invasion), than 'Linear A' found everywhere in Crete put together.

There is a rather complicated aspect to Mycenaean origins which is important, particularly in the context of the argument that Greek civilization has its foundations in the Near East. It is suggested that Mycenaeans were not an Aryan people. Like the Cretans, they were a Mediterranean dark-white race. One school of thought shows that their original home was along the north-western littoral of Asia Minor, while that of the Minoans was the coastal-plain of Syria-Palestine.

Those who believe that the Mycenaeans originated from Asia Minor, remind us that they were later identified as the Achaeans of Homer's *Iliad*, and with Troy in north-western Asia Minor. Adjoining the western frontiers of the Hittites, (see chapter 7), there was a powerful kingdom called Ahhiyawa. The reader will note the phonetic similarity between 'Achaea' and 'Ahhiyawa'. But according to some scholarly assessment, this similarity is coincidental.[11] Yet others 'fully agree' with the theory that Achaeans and Ahhiyawa are identical.[12] However, one keeps an open mind on such problems relating to the remote times under discussion.

In view of suggestions quoted below it must be stated that although the Hittite texts name Ahhiyawa for the first time c. 1350, that does not necessarily mean that the citizens of Ahhiyawa were not already in their homeland in western Asia Minor long before that time.

> Archaeologists, finding that the Ahhiyawa homeland can be located on the Anatolian mainland without violating any logical inference from the texts, have recently begun to favour a new theory regarding this north-western province.[13]

According to this theory, the Ahhiyawans themselves

> appeared from the west simultaneously with the arrival of the Hittites from the east. By this process of reasoning, the Ahhiyawans would have been a proto-Greek people who remained on the Anatolian mainland during the centuries in which their own colonists were creating the Mycenaean commune in the Aegean. This would explain the close ties between the Mycenaean merchants and the Trojans of the sixth settlement.[14]

Those Ahhiyawan emigrants from Asia Minor could be described as the Mycenaean colonists who settled in the south of the Peloponnese, and perhaps retained their original name, 'Ahhiyawa' in a modified form, 'Achaea'. These 'Achaea' were themselves invaded by a new wave of Asiatics, possibly more of their Ahhiyawan cousins, who adopted for themselves the name of the country they seized, Mycenaea, from where they expelled the first settlers. The latter, the Achaeans, were forced to

> retreat to the mountainous northern coastal regions of the Peloponnese, which retained the name, Achaia, into later times, while others took refuge on the east coast of Attica and Euboia and the islands.[15]

In such circumstances, the Trojan war, between Homer's 'Achaio' and the Mycenaeans could be seen as a fratricidal war.

It is extremely difficult to offer dates for these changes. There is, however, one anchorage around which an assessment might be acceptable. We know that the Mycenaeans (who, as suggested above, ousted the Achaeans) were actively trading with the Minoans certainly in the seventeenth century probably c.1650. They, as well as the original settlers who were driven north, appear to be the *Achaio* of Homer, whose kings built a maritime empire held together by tributary rulers. The centre of that empire could have been not Mycenae in the Peloponnese but Ahhiyawa in western Asia Minor:

> Perhaps there lies some truth behind the legend that Pelops and his followers came to Mycenae from Lydia, then called the country of Arzawa.[16]

Other refugees from the Greek mainland also overflowed into Anatolia, where the important city of Miletus was founded. 'The whole area is to be identified with that kingdom of Ahhiyawa which was so well known to the Hittites.' (c.1350)[17] According to tradition yet more natives of mainland Greece took refuge in Asia Minor from later invaders (probably the Dorians (c.1200)) and founded Smyrna, Ephesus and the other "Ionian" city states.

> At this point we should perhaps remind ourselves that, by the time the Achaean Greeks organized the expedition against the city of Troy described by Homer, the events mentioned in the Hittite records were already becoming historical. The best known date, computed by the Greek chronologists of later times, for the fall of Troy (and one which most archaeologists find most easy to accept), is 1192 BC.[18]

The above is a simplified account of an extremely complex subject which is still fluid and much argued and discussed by scholars. A recent suggestion refers to

> two crucial texts being once more dated to the end of the fifteenth century BC . . . the recent reappraisal of the texts shows that the Hittite king treated on terms of equality with the ruler of Ahhiyawa, who was also a Great King and whose brother was stationed at Millawanda as his representative on Anatolian soil. It is therefore likely that Ahhiyawa was located on the Greek mainland, that Millawanda was indeed Miletus.[19]

My outline of the histories of Babylonia, Egypt, Crete and the Mycenaeans came down as far as the appearance of the Sea Peoples at the end of the Bronze Age (c.1200.), a time of great changes. We find Mycenaeans or, as Homer calls them in the *Iliad*, the Achaioi (Achaeans) – a non-Greek name – making war against Troy (c.1192), an important city-state, or perhaps, as suggested by a scholar, 'western Asia Minor at the time of the Trojan War.'[20]

While the Trojan war was being fought the Peloponnese was invaded by the Aryan Dorians, the historical Greeks,

> the first people of Greek speech to enter the south of Greece (from the region

of Epirus) came, not as the creators but as the destroyers of the Mycenaean world, at the very end of the Bronze Age a generation or so before 1200 BC. [21]
That Dorian invasion and that Trojan war took place about the time and as part of the raids of the Sea Peoples (see chapter 8).

The final historical result of this complex period of many changes is that the Aegean cultures were those of Crete, influenced by the Asiatic and Egyptian legacies, which were transported to the Greek mainland, by the Mycenaeans and the Minoans themselves, to be added to the store of knowledge which had been accumulating on that mainland for many centuries, by the efforts of the natives themselves, helped by travellers and immigrants from Asia Minor, via the Cyclades and, later, from the Ionian 'colonies'.

Notes

1. Caskey John L., 'Greece, Crete and the Agean Islands in the Early Bronze Age', *CAH I²* pp. 800-2.
2. Hall H. R., *The Ancient History of the Near East*, Methuen, London, 1963.
3. Hood Sinclair, *The Home of the Heroes*, Thames & Hudson, London 1974.
4. Hood Sinclair, *The Home of the Heroes, op.cit.*
5. Matz F., 'The Maturity of Minoan Civilization', *CAH II¹*, pp. 162-3.
6. Hood Sinclair, *The Home of the Heroes, op.cit.*pp. 106, 108.
7. Hall H. R., *The Ancient History of the Near East*, Methuen, London, 1963.
8. Hall H. R., *ibid.*
9. Hall H. R., *ibid.*
10. Hood Sinclair, *The Home of the Heroes, op.cit*, pp. 106. 108.
11. Lloyd Seton, *Ancient Turkey*, British Museum Publications, London, 1989, p.54
12. Itamar Singer, 'Western Anatolia in the 13th Century BC'. *AS XXXIII*, p. 206.
13. Lloyd Seton, *Early Highland Peoples of Anatolia*, Thames & Hudson, London, 1967, p. 80.
14. Lloyd Seton, *Ibid.*
15. Mellaart James, 'Anatolian Trade Geography and Culture in Late Bronze Age', *AS XIII*, p. 195.
16. Desborough R d'A, 'The End of the Mycenean Civilization and the Dark Ages', *CAH II²*, p. 658.
17. Lloyd Seton, *Early Highland Peoples of Anatolia, op.cit.*
18. Lloyd Seton, *ibid.*
19. Lloyd Seton, *Ancient Turkey*, British Museum, London, 1989, p. 54.
20. Lloyd Seton, *ibid.*
21. Hood Sinclair, *The Home of the Heroes, op. cit.* p. 126; Hall H.R., *The Ancient History of the Near East, op. cit.*, p. 78.

Chapter 7
Anatolia

HITTITES AND HURRIANS: Before re-entering Asia and continuing to narrate the complex events that followed the decline of Babylon as an imperial power, it would be useful to recapitulate, very briefly, on some of the salient events told in the previous chapters, after the rise of the Mesopotamian city states.

The important rule of the great *entrepôt* ports, on the coast of Syria-Palestine, has been cited. These served central and eastern Anatolian traders as well as those from Mesopotamia. In the south, Sidon and Tyre were ancient Canaanite-Phoenician cities, in which there would have been (as in many other Levantine towns) a community of Mycenaeans and Minoans, who no doubt added their own considerable traditions of seafaring to those of the Phoenicians themselves. It is suggested that Mycenaean merchants persuaded some Phoenicians to abandon their exclusive, age-old, secure, very active trading with Egypt and the Levantine countries, to venture, with Mycenaean seamen, to the western Mediterranean and even beyond the Pillars of Hercules.[1]

The prosperity of the great sea ports implies a busy, ongoing exchange of goods between all the states along the banks of the Euphrates and the Tigris: Sumer-Akkad, Babylon and Assyria, to and from Cyprus (with its deposits of copper), Egypt, Crete, Greece, Mycenae and other lands towards the west. The great riverine highways also continued to serve Mesopotamian merchants to expand their flourishing trade with the peoples of the Anatolian highlands. After c.2000, a prosperous trade would have been carried on, along the east-west valleys of Anatolia, with the Hittites and the states adjoining them: Ahhiyawa, Arzawa, Kizzuwatna, and others, also (after c.1200) the Ionian city states, along the Mediterranean littoral, whose merchants were themselves doing business with mainland Greece.

Trade would be conducted irrespective of the ambitions and fortunes of kings and princes. Merchants are not inhibited by the political idiosyncrasies of their rulers, so long as the trade routes are reasonably open in wartime, which in those days they probably were. Unlike modern wars, the effects of which are so widespread, in ancient, and even in medieval times, caravans might bypass armies and battlefields; ships could sail on the high seas, and in wartime it would have been only marginally more dangerous than in peacetime, when there was always the possibility of an encounter with pirates. Indeed, it can be truly said that generally it was often in the material interests of the battling kings not to interfere with trade, unless their armies actually encountered enemy caravans which they could legitimately seize – and all honour to the legal robbers.

Business methods were much advanced, even as early as, and before, Hammurabi's times (c.2000). Goods which were unobtainable in Mesopotamia – such as timber, building-stone and metals – were imported from Anatolia, down the rivers, and from Elam, the Zagros mountains in the east and beyond. Payment was by barter of Mesopotamian products – Assyrian textiles, and skilfully and artistically fashioned craft-ware of the south, lapis lazuli from Afghanistan and perhaps re-routing of goods from India (Mohenjo-Daro, Harappa) by land and sea. The function of promissory notes and the commercial knowledge of dealings in 'futures' were well known.

We have seen how Hammurabi of Babylon (1792-1750) disciplined the ambitious nobles and princelings within his inheritance, and having established social justice by his Code of laws, witnessed economic growth within a stable social order. Assyria, with its capital, Ashur, to the north of Babylon, had been gathering strength under king Shamshi-Adad I (1813-1781), from a line of kings or more probably chieftains, of non-Assyrian, Semite-nomadic, origin. From his capital he controlled vast territories in the west, and threatened Babylon. Hammurabi attacked and destroyed the great city of Mari (whose viceroy was Shamshi-Adad's son) as well as Ashur itself, thus curbing Assyrian ambitions.

Hammurabi's reign marked the zenith of power of the Babylonian Empire, which went into a decline after his death (1750). Then, the city of Babylon was attacked and destroyed by the Hittite king Mursili. After his departure, Babylonia was briefly occupied by the Gutians, who were followed by the Sealanders. That unstable situation opened the way for the Kassites who seized Babylon, adopted its religion and culture, and established a new Kassite dynasty (c.1590) which lasted as a considerable power for 500 years.

THE HITTITES AND THE MITANNI: We have now come full circle back into Asia. The homelands of the Aryan peoples extended from the Aral Sea region in Central Asia to the western end of the northern coast of the Black Sea. It is increasingly accepted that a nomadic tribe who eventually became known as the Hittites, with Aryan speech, having travelled along the northern side of the Black Sea penetrated Anatolia from the west, over the Bosphorus, and even from the south into northern Syria. We find them ultimately as a powerful unit threatening the Assyrian trading stations (Karum) in the vicinity of the river Halys. Other Aryan hordes penetrated eastern Anatolia from around Lake Urmia, the Caucasus and the Zagros mountains c.2500. The wave of newcomers from the Lakes Urmia-Van region is recognised as the important Hurrian people, the Horites of the Bible (Gen.XIV.6; Deut.II.12) with a speech which had traces of Aryan but still described as 'agglutinative'.[2] They emerged in loose tribal communities and settled in eastern and central Anatolia and northern Mesopotamia. The original eastern Anatolian settlements around Lake Van, later developed into the powerful, pre-Armenian (pre-600 BC) kingdom of Urartu or Ararat. Other Hurrians (a ubiquitous people) scattered in groups of varying sizes in many parts of the Near East, appeared even among the Hyksos and in Babylonia. The Aryan, horse-riding Mitanni appeared from beyond the Zagros mountains and spread westwards into northern Mesopotamia where they settled as a ruling aristocracy over Hurrian tribes.

THE HITTITES: Until the first half of the nineteenth century AD, 'Hittite' was the Biblical name for an unknown people who inhabited Syria and perhaps Asia Minor. When, however, in the 1860's AD strange pictographic inscriptions on rock faces were found in the north of the Taurus, which were comparable to similar inscriptions found earlier carved on basalt slabs in northern Syria, the validity of the Biblical stories of the Hittites was accepted. The inscriptions when deciphered, proved their authors to be the people called the Khetta (the Hittites) by the Egyptians. They are mentioned by the scribes of Tuthmoses III (fifteenth century) and in Rameses II's treaty of Kadesh (1269) of which a copy was found at the archaeological site of Boghaz Köy at the bend of the Halys river. There were also the Amarna letters in cuneiform, one of which was from the king of the Hittites, Shuppiluliumas, from his capital Hattusa (Boghaz Köy), to Amunhotep III. These factors support the most recent of scholarly opinion that those who were later identified with the Hittites first appeared in the Near East in northern Syria, as suggested above.

The important discovery in 1906, at Boghaz Köy, of a vast library of cuneiform tablets, which included the Hittite version of the Treaty of Kadesh, became the foundations for piecing together the history of the Hittites. They had one of the most ancient of the Indo-European languages. Their features are described as Armenoid, and, in fact they do closely resemble Armenian features, with prominent nose and receding chin.[3] Recent findings show that, having traversed the northern side of the Black Sea, they entered Anatolia over the Bosphorus.[4] Some could have continued their journey southward into northern Syria. As from about 1870 BC. names found in the Kanesh (modern Kültepe) tablets show that the peoples of Mesopotamia from the period of Akkad and Babylon to Assyria, not only traded but also intermarried with the indigenous Anatolian Hattian (not Hittite) people and, later, with the newcomers with Indo-European names as well. The Hittites adopted the Hattian name. One of the most important of those texts with names is that found in the ruined native Hattian palace on the mound of Kanesh. It has the name of Anittas[5] who lived before the rise of the Hittite kingdom. He appears to have been the last of the indigenous kings.

The Hittites infiltrated the Assyrian trading station at Kültepe (Kanesh). Among its ruins, dating from the Assyrian presence there, a tablet seems to foreshadow the unchallengeable rule of the Hittite kings. Indeed, they ousted the native Hattians from Kanesh and ended Hattian history, although they adopted the Hattian name for themselves, together with certain basic traditions of their subjects. The beginning of this Hittite predominance in western Anatolia is dated at about 1660 and the recorded history of the Anatolian peninsula is mainly that of the Hittite kingdom.

Briefly, the Aryan people who became known as the Hittites, crossed the Bosphorus. They infiltrated, then appropriated the Assyrian trading posts (*Karum*), in central Anatolia, including the most important one at Kanesh (Kültepe). They settled in the bend of the River Halys, where they adopted the name of the indigenous people, the 'Hattians' or 'Hatti', 'Khatti'. In time, they were masters of, or wielded a powerful influence over the kingdoms or principalities in the whole region, from the Aegean to the Euphrates, even breaking through the Taurus mountains and colonising the important area of Carchemish at the crossing of the Euphrates (if it was not already occupied by other Hittites who had crossed into Syria after crossing the Bosphorus), which was to become, after the twelfth century, the small, but important, so called neo-Hittite state, whose people were the Biblical Hittites (The Children of Heth, Gen. XXIII.3).

The already tenuous communications of the Assyrian *karum* in Anatolia with their homeland (which had become a Mitannian colony) were completely cut off after the arrival of the Hittites, who destroyed their trade, making their settlements economic redundancies. The Hittites had sought to obtain the tin, which had been available to their Assyrian predecessors via Ashur, from the eastern highlands and the Urmia region[6], but the appearance of the Mitanni had frustrated that plan.

However, that essential element in the production of bronze (an admixture of about 7% tin to copper) could still be obtained from (a) near Nigde, modern south-central Turkey;[7] (b) a tin mine at the foot of Mount Aragatz, Armenia;[8] and (c) Bohemian mines in the west.[9] Hittite policy was always to persuade, either by military threat or diplomacy, the Arzawa states and Ahhiyawa in western Asia Minor, to keep open the trade route between eastern Europe and central Anatolia.

Not satisfied with the already huge extent of his territories, the Hittite King took advantage of the collapse of the Egyptian Twelfth Dynasty (1786) whose friendly relations with some distant, great Syrian city-states, such as Ugarit and Yamkhad, had evaporated during the Second Intermediate Period (c.1800-1600).[10] He broke through the passes of the Taurus, and seized the powerful kingdom of Aleppo. King Mursili I (1620-1590) inherited Northern Syria, destroyed Aleppo, presumably to obviate rebellion, and descended upon and, as stated above, sacked Babylon (1590). On his return to Hattusa, his capital, he was murdered by his brother-in-law. During the struggle for power in Hattusa, Syria was seized by the Mitanni and soon the southern trade routes were closed to the Hittites.

THE MITANNI. In the sixteenth century an important horse-riding, chariot-owning aristocracy, with Aryan names and Indian or Vedic gods – Mitra, Varuna, Indra – appeared in northern Mesopotamia where they colonised the Semitic city of Nuzi (south of the river Zab, near Kirkuk). They built a temple where 4,000 cuneiform tablets were discovered recording their legal, social and business affairs. By the fifteenth century, the Aryan Mitanni had welded the Hurrian settlements in northern Mesopotamia into the kingdom of Mitanni, had imposed their rule upon Semitic Assyria and created an empire stretching from Kurdistan and the Zagros to Harran and the Mediterranean. From 1500 to 1360 all the Assyrian kings were vassals of Mitanni; when one of them dared to revolt, Saussatar, King of Mitanni, plundered the capital, Ashur, and took away 'a door of silver and gold' and installed it in his own capital, Washukkanni. Assyria was in subjection until at least the time of king Ashur-Uballit (c.1365-1330).

Mitannian horsemanship and horse-drawn, two-wheeled chariots imply the training of horses. Mitannian-Hurrian textbooks describe methods of breaking horses and training them, even for racing. The various technical terms have Aryan forms which show the oriental origin both of the Mitanni and their small Asiatic horse.[11] Horses were in use in the fifteenth century by the aristocratic Mitanni and introduced by them to the neighbouring Hittites in Anatolia, and (somewhat later) they were harnessed to the chariots of the Egyptian pharaohs. But they were not available to ordinary people, who used the onager (a kind of wild ass) and the donkey, until after the thirteenth century. Mitannian, contemporary Kassite and later Assyrian military power depended upon those essential techniques and skills of horsemanship, which introduced important changes in military strategy. Another significant factor showing the Aryan origin of the Mitanni was their tradition of cremating their early kings. These factors support the view that an Aryan warrior caste ruled over a mainly non-Aryan, Hurrian people.

Mitannian rule spread into Syria, even as far south as Lebanon. The Phoenician cities retained their political independence and took care of their commercial relationships across the Levant, with Egypt and Cilicia (southern Anatolia) in the west and Babylonia in the east. Canaan and Phoenicia were vulnerable to possible Egyptian invasion from the south and Hittite or Mitannian attacks from the north; the Kassites in Babylonia were too far to come to their aid.

Having expelled the Asiatic Hyksos (c.1570), Egyptian policy changed from one of isolation between two great deserts, to an aggressive invasion of western Asia. All three powers (Khatti (or Hatti – Hittites), Mitanni, Egypt) coveted the wealthy Taurus foothills of northern Syria and its traditional, highly profitable, coastal entrepôt trade with the Levant, Mesopotamia and central and eastern Anatolia.

The Amarna Tablets are our main source of knowledge on the kingdom of Mitanni. Although these begin only after 1450, when Mitanni was already an established and powerful state in northern Mesopotamia, a number of Aryan names are to be found in the Egyptian archives pre-dating 1450 which might be the names of earlier Mitannian kings. Parattarna was the first historically credible king of Mitanni (c.1500). We know of him as the ruler of a kingdom in northern Mesopotamia and tribute paying states in Syria. His power was equal to those of Egypt and Hatti respectively. He was followed by Saussatar who remained on good terms with Egypt's Tuthmoses III (1479-1421), in spite of the latter's incursions into Mitanni's Hurrian territories in Syria. Saussatar was succeeded by Artatama, who gave his daughter in marriage to Tuthmoses IV (1413-1405), an unprecedented event – the marriage of an Egyptian king to a Mitannian princess – which was followed by other marriages between princesses of Mitanni and Pharaohs Amunhotep III and Akhenaten. The latter married the beautiful princess Nefertiti, perhaps the daughter of king Shutarna II of Mitanni (c.1380).

> Under these kings Mitanni still controlled Assyria, and Artatama apparently was able to employ an Assyrian deity, Ishtar of Nineveh, to increase his credit at the Egyptian court; a letter to Amenophis (Amunhotep) III from Artatama's grandson Tushratta, announcing that Ishtar of Nineveh had expressed a desire to visit the Egyptian court again, refers to a former visit of the statue in the time of one of Tushratta's predecesors. Obviously Ishtar of Nineveh had a high reputation internationally, which must certainly have reflected lustre upon her guardians.[12]

Ishtar in a number of guises – Queen of Heaven, Earth goddess, Love goddess – had indeed been worshipped down the ages by many peoples and under various names.

These demonstrations of friendship between Egypt and Mitanni were in addition to the extensive trade and cultural influence between the two kingdoms. Mitanni straddled the important Fertile Crescent trade route in the north and controlled the tribute-paying port of Alalakh, and indirectly the great port of Ugarit (Ras Shamra). Both ports traded regularly with Egypt, as with other lands, across the Levantine and the Aegean seas. The Aegean peoples, for example, traded extensively with Europe importing, among other luxury items, amber from the north, via the Adriatic Sea.

Minoan and Egyptian influence can be detected in the design and colouring of pottery of Alalakh, which depicts papyrus and lotus stems. Alalakh vases, standing on slender feet, are more elegant than any other produced in the Near East until that time. Mitannian kings are represented in copper statuettes, wearing broad-bordered cloaks, typical of the Hurri-Mitanni region. Most interesting of all, according to Egyptian accounts, Mitanni traded in willow, ash and horn-beam, from the Amanus mountains, which they shipped to Egypt for making light chariots.

The greatest of Hittite kings, Shuppiluliumas I (c.1380-1349) mounted an abortive attack upon Mitanni in an attempt to seize the northern ports of Syria. Ultimately he achieved this by subduing Mitanni's northern allies of Isuwa and Kizzuwatna, quickly occupying territories west of the Euphrates; then directly attacking and occupying Aleppo, thus firmly establishing Hittite rule once more at the head of the Euphrates route. He strengthened his position by marrying a Babylonian princess.[13]

Having sufficiently reinforced his power, Shuppiluliumas invaded Mitanni, captured its wealthy capital, Washukkanni, and destroyed much of its remaining power. Finally he attacked and subdued Karchemish, the vigorous state situated at the crossing of the Euphrates, nearest to the Mediterranean coast, which perpetuated Hittite supremacy in north Syria. He precluded potential Hittite danger by using his subject, Mitanni, as a buffer-state. As already narrated, even Egypt almost became a sphere of Hittite influence, when Tutankhamun's young widow (or, according to some scholars, Nefertiti herself) asked for the hand in marriage of one of Shuppiluliumas' sons. *En route*, to his marriage to a daughter and wife of kings and pharaohs, the murder of that prince, averted a possible disaster for ancient Egypt.

After his death, Shuppiluliumas was succeeded by his son, Mursili II, whose priority appears to have been the successful consolidation of his father's enormous empire in Anatolia. At the end, he had to face the might of Egypt under its young and exuberant Pharaoh Rameses II. Mursili died of old age, and was succeeded by his son Muwatallis who seems to have been an astute young man. He realised, like his father, that sooner or later there would be a great battle between the two empires for supremacy over the whole of the Near East.

Pharaoh Rameses II (1290-1224), with his great army and shining regiment of light chariots, headed for north Syria and forced a clash between Egypt and Khatti near the city of Kadesh, on the river Orontes (1285).

This is one of history's great, decisive and well-documented battles. Rameses claimed victory and made a triumphant return to his capital. In fact the battle was nearly a draw, and really in favour of the Hittites, who retained control of northern Syria. But, in the midst of the Hittite king's preoccupation with his Egyptian war, Assyria successfully attacked Mitanni and made it its vassal.

Then, it is a history of conspiracy and intrigue in the Hittite capital for the succession, following the death of King Muwatallis (c.1284). In the long series of family feuds, the western part of the Hittite empire disappeared and Hattusil, brother of Muwatallis, emerged as king over no more than the regions of the original homelands. Hattusa and Egypt, in the face of a threatening Assyria, which had shaken off the domination of both Babylon and Mitanni, signed a non-aggression pact, said to be the first of its kind – the Treaty of Kadesh (1269). Two copies of the Treaty, one in each language, were signed. This demarcated Egypt's sphere as far as, and including Palestine. Each side was to aid the other in case of need. Five years later Rameses III married Hatusille III's daughter.

Assyria's King Shalmaneser I (1275-1245) now (1275) free from threat or restraint from his country's old adversaries, Babylon, Khatti or Egypt, destroyed Mitanni for ever. Its king Saussatar fled from the battlefield with his aristocracy, leaving 14,000 of his subjects to be blinded by the Assyrian conqueror. Hittite communications with the south were cut off, except for the island of Cyprus and its rich copper mines, which could still be used as a stepping-stone to Syria.

Even in such a brief survey as this, something must be written on the social organisation of the Hittites, particularly as their principles of land distribution, applied almost down to this day throughout Anatolia. There were very few 'cities'. The one which could, with conviction be given that title was the capital, Hattusa, on today's archaeological site of Boghaz Köy. The rest were more like villages, each divided from its neighbour by a strip of land. The village and the land on which it stood, were owned in common by the inhabitants, some of whom worked on the land and cultivated food.

The craftsmen-artists and artisans bartered their wares and skills for their own necessities. The headmen of each village saw to the execution of the laws of the community.

The position of women seems to have been largely liberal. 'A king's wife could be queen in her own right.'[14] A man could give away his daughter in marriage, as he could in Western Europe down to the end of the nineteenth century, AD. But Hittite wives seem to have enjoyed somewhat greater independence than their nineteenth century British counterparts. They

> had at least some say in the disposal of their daughters in marriage and, in certain circumstances (admittedly very obscure) they could disown their sons and even divorce their husbands. Although the normal marriage arrangement was that a man 'took' a wife and 'made a house and children' with her ... it was possible in some cases for a woman to remain in her father's house after marriage. On the other hand the custom of levirate marriage, by which a widow was married to her late husband's brother, father or other surviving male relative, can only have been acceptable in a society where male primacy was a recognised feature.[15]

There were slaves in Khatti, as everywhere else in the ancient world.

> The extra manpower they provided was increasingly needed, in the Imperial period (1450-1200), when Hittite citizens were increasingly required for military duties, yet improved productivity was demanded at the same time.[16]

The king, of course, was supreme and the country's code of laws and traditions were protected by the aristocracy, whose interest it was to support him. Unlike the Assyrians and the ancient traditions, their diplomacy appeared to take precedence over brute force. In their view, it was better to solve a difference with other states by suitable concessions or by a marriage of members of the respective royal families.

Their religion and its rites seem to have been more modest, less grandiose, than those of other great kingdoms of the times. They believed in the most primitive aspect of the Mother-goddess, Arinna, followed by the Nature gods and goddesses. The Mother represented the ever-thirsty Earth which could not be quenched, and she could not conceive without the power and fecundity of the Water and Weather God, Tarhunda, for whom there were temples and open-air shrines, especially where there were springs, as at Yazilikaya. They were remembered and worshipped particularly at agricultural seasonal festivals. And, of course, there was a hierarchy of other gods and goddesses and many superstitions. Fear of the Unknown, generated by incomprehensible natural phenomena and the dark future, would be assuaged by medicine men, witches and magicians. The king was the deputy, chief priest and intermediary of the Storm god and Mother-goddess, and his duties to his people purported to be the commands of the deities. Unlike the Egyptian Pharaoh he was not god incarnate.

As to their art, it is interesting that it could be described as being, like their religion, seldom powerful. Indeed, if such Hittite art as remains were taken out of its environment and the context of its history, it would be, with few exceptions, of little value. However, within the context of the region in which it is found, the walls of palaces and temples on which it is sculptured, and the history with which it is associated, it is of great interest, particularly because of the paucity of examples. It does show us their stature, their clothing, their stance and the implications of some of their ceremonies. Outstanding examples of the few extant figures in the round are those of the 'portal-figures of two lions adorning a gateway to the outer city (Hattusa) at Boghaz Köy.'[17] There are also the arresting sculptures in relief of gods and goddesses, embellishing the sanctuary, cut out of the rock at Yazilikaya, not far from Boghaz Köy, where there is a generous spring, as at other Hittite religious centres. The city of Hattusa was surrounded by massive walls and it was large enough to invite the folk in the villages nearby to take shelter in it, during time of war.

Finally, at the end of this chapter, I should restate that it seems to be generally agreed that it was through the Mitanni, via the Hittites, that the complex pattern of ideas of Mesopotamian civilization travelled to the western coast of Asia Minor and thence, over the Cyclades, to mainland Greece. The first important manifestations of that influence appeared in the Ionian city states (see chapter 8) on the west coast of Asia Minor at the end of the Bronze Age (c.1200), which also witnessed the destruction of the Hittite Empire.

Notes

1. Woolley Leonard, *Mesopotamia*, London, 1961.

2. Dower Margaret S., 'Syria 1550-1400 BC', *CAH II¹*, p. 418.

3. Renfrew Colin, *Archaeology and Language*, Jonathan Cape, London, 1987.

4. Lloyd Seton, *Ancient History of Anatolia*, British Museum Publications, 1989.

5. Gurney O.R., *The Hittites*, Pelican Books, London, 1954.

6. Posner G., 'Syria and Palestine, c. 2610-1780 BC', CAH I², pp. 548-9.

7. Gurney O.R., *The Hittites*, Pelican Books, London, 1954, p. 96.

8. Mellaart James, 'Anatolian Trade, Geography and Culture', AS XVIII, 1969, pp. 188, 200.

9. Macqueen J.G., 'Geography and History in Asia Minor in 2nd Millenium BC', *AS XIII*.

10 Posner G., *op. cit.*

11. Oates Joan, *Babylon*, Thames & Hudson, London, 1979, p. 87.

12. Saggs W.H.T., *The Greatness that was Babylon*, Sidgwick & Jackson, London, 1969, p. 79.

13. Macqueen J.G., *The Hittites*, Thames & Hudson, London, 1975, p. 45.

14. Lloyd Seton, *Ancient History of Anatolia, op. cit.* p. 50.

15. Macqueen J.G., *op. cit.* pp. 43, 113.

16. *ibid.*

17. Lloyd Seton, *Early Highland Peoples of Anatolia*, Thames & Hudson, London, 1967.

Chapter 8
The Sea Peoples

An approximate date, 1200 BC, is proposed to divide the Bronze Age from the Iron Age. It is a watershed in the ancient history of the Near East. By that time the most ancient civilizations in southern and central Mesopotamia, Sumer-Akkad-Babylon in turn, had had their day: the powerful Mitanni, which had controlled northern Mesopotamia and Syria, was annihilated by Assyria (c.1275). The arts, literature, systems of law and the culture generally of those most ancient peoples had been handed down in ever more intricate forms to meet the needs of increasingly complex social patterns. It was mainly the Mitanni who had transmitted Babylonian civilization to the Hittites, and so westwards to Ionia and ultimately to Greece. Most importantly, the Phoenicians used the Egyptian hieroglyphics to construct an alphabet for themselves, consisting only of consonants, which was later adopted by the Greeks who added the vowels. That alphabet no doubt ultimately aided the rapid rise of Greek civilization.

The technology of smelting iron had been developing in eastern Anatolia, especially at the mound of Metsamore, west of modern Erevan, where tribes of Hurrian-Urartians, the predecessors of the Armenians (pre-600 BC) had settled long before c.2100 BC. That area and the Chalybes (a Hittite colony) were connected to Hatti by the kingdom of Hayasa-Azzi. The two kingdoms had much trading and social intercourse with one another. The knowledge of iron smelting could have easily reached the Hittites over those territories. Also, closely connected with the introduction of iron to the Near East, were the horse-riding Mitanni, who must have passed through the wide-spread Urartian tribal lands, including eastern Urmia, and possibly captured some prisoners, including some ironmasters, and taken them to their ultimate settlements in northern Mesopotamia. By the fifteenth century, the northern frontiers of defunct Mitanni were contiguous with the Hittite kingdom and Hurri-Urartian areas. The powerful Hatti seized the important Mitannian iron-smelting centre of Kizzuwatna, to the west of the Euphrates, in southern Anatolia. Thus, in the fourteenth century, the smelting of iron became almost a Hittite monopoly. As Hittite influence was very widespread, it is not surprising that peoples to the south and west of that kingdom, including those beyond the Hellespont, gradually acquired the technology of iron-smelting and the uses to which that strong, solid metal could be put. Iron weapons of war, such as spears and arrowheads were far superior to the bronze ones. In time, cheap iron tools, such as plough-shares and tools for reclaiming wasteland, became available, making the small producers more independent from state monopolies and the aristocracies. Vehicles and iron components of ships offered faster transport and more reliable communications. The increasing use of iron, as from c.1000 BC, made its production ever more sophisticated, cheaper and ultimately universal. Strangely, however, the Assyrians, close neighbours of the Hittites, do not seem to have used iron until well into the ninth century.

The late thirteenth century was a period of great international confusion. Egypt's most glorious centuries were past. The illustrious New Kingdom was approaching its end. The royal Amunhoteps had given place to the powerful second and third of the Ramesids. Rameses III ruled early in the twelfth century (1196-1166). There are migrations of little known peoples. The earliest ones are recorded by the scribes of Pharaoh Meneptah (1236-1223), who write of Egypt's victory, in 1232, over 'peoples of the sea.' They were Libyans, supported by sea-faring northerners, such as the Teresh, the Lukka, the Sherdane (possibly the Sardinians) of whom we know very little. They were refugees and adventurers seeking fertile lands, new homes, rich cities to despoil. Some groups could even be described as organised military and naval units invading established city-states and kingdoms.

There is trouble in Anatolia and the Levant: among tablets from Ugarit, three letters mention famine in Khatti.

> Ugarit is asked to send 2,000 measures of grain to Cilicia. But a letter from the king of Ugarit appeals for help to the king of Alashiya (Cyprus), who urges Ugarit to arm a fleet of 150 ships to resist the enemy. Ugarit, writing again to Cyprus, says that 'all my forces and chariots are stationed in Khatti Land, and all my ships in Lukka Land; seven enemy ships have appeared and inflicted much damage upon us.[1]

So the combined fleets of Khatti, Ugarit and Alashiya are massing off Lycia, while their armies are joining up in the west. Towards the end of the reign of Shuppiluliumas II (c. 1215), the last Hittite king, Alashiya had changed sides and its ships were fighting against the Hittites. The Alashiya fleet was defeated, set alight and destroyed.

These events were the prelude to the invasions of peoples who appeared in Asia Minor from across European Thrace, over the Bosphorus and the river Sangarius (c.1190), looting and setting alight towns and villages, killing those who opposed them, welcoming into their own ranks those who proved their military prowess. Chief among these emigrants were the Phrygians (Bruges), referred to by the Assyrians (wrongly) as Mushki (or Kashka, from the south Pontus region). The Ahhiyawa must have been the first to be displaced by them as were, in consequence, most of the peoples in western and south-western Anatolia, except the Luwians of the western plateau who withstood them and eventually formed the kingdoms of Lydia and Lycia.[2] Probably aided by the Mushki and others, Hattusa was put to the torch and the powerful Hittite Empire was expunged, causing the displacement of many neighbouring peoples. The trade routes collapsed. The various remaining states in western Anatolia which were, at least nominally, subject to, or on friendly diplomatic terms with their great neighbour, the Hittite Empire, lost their identities and were replaced by the

Figure 28. A lioness mauling an African. Ivory covered plaque covered with gold leaf and inlaid with lapis lazuli and cornelian. Ninth - eighth century BC, from Nimrud (Calah). Ht. 10.35cm. Courtesy, Trustees of the British Museum.

newcomers.

Among the surviving states in western Anatolia, the Luwians formed the Kingdoms of Lydia and Lycia.[3] They suffered with other states in the region a great famine, lasting 18 years. An obscure people in Lydia, the Etruscans, fled and sailed from Smyrna to their new home in Italy (c.1000 BC), where eventually they founded a powerful kingdom which survived until the coming of the Romans.

While the Phrygians remained the successors of the Hittites, many others, (with their families, womenfolk, wives, children followed) in solid, four-wheeled, heavy waggons, drawn by humped oxen, crossed the Taurus into Syria and Palestine. Their fleet kept pace with them. Karchemish, Aleppo, Alalakh and wealthy Ugarit were razed; the Amorite kingdom of Syria was wiped out. Across the water, they wasted Cyprus, and Rhodes was occupied probably by the Akawasha-Ahhiyawan-Achaeans-Mycenaeans, who appear to be a ubiquitous race of pirates and parasites, some of whom had established stable kingdoms such as those in north-west Anatolia, in southern Peloponnesus and Crete. Others of their race plied the seas as raiders and rovers, much as some of the Homeric heroes did on their way home after the Trojan war. Other refugee Achaeans

Figure 29. Ashurnasirpal II, King of Assyria (884-859 BC) in court dress. Stone bas-relief. From Numrud (Calah). Courtesy, Trustees of the British Museum.

(Ahhiyawa), now turned pirates, assisted the Libyans by land and sea. Egypt was attacked for the second time. The Philistines (the Pulesti or Peleset), Aryan raiders who might first have appeared in Crete, tried to seize Egypt.

That second invasion by land and sea was thrown back by Rameses III (1198-1166) and utterly destroyed by his well-manned navy, his great army and swift chariots, supported by rank upon rank of bowmen, to kill the aggressors, who carried long, iron spears, before they came too close for hand-to-hand fighting. That *tour de force* revivified Egypt which survived for yet another 1000 years, albeit under foreign dynasties, including a Libyan one (c.950-730). The defeated

Figure 30. Colossal human-headed winged bull. From the palace of King Ashurnasirpal II of Assyria (884-859 BC) at Nimrud. Courtesy, Trustees of the British Museum.

Philistines, driven off to the western littoral of the land of the Canaanites, were allowed to settle there. Thenceforth that country was known as 'Palestine'.

A fierce Aryan people, known as the Dorians (the true Greeks: see chapter 6), from the northern Balkan lands and Epirus, overran Greece, and descended into the Peloponnesus, where they destroyed the Mycenaean power (possibly just when the main Mycenaean armies and fleet were involved in the *Iliad's* Trojan war). They sacked Nestor's palace at Pylos and destroyed the great citadel of Mycenae itself. In their fierce onslaught down the Greek mainland, they displaced the Aeolians and the Ionians, who fled to the Aegean islands and the western litoral of Anatolia, where they founded flourishing cities such as Phocaea,

Figure 31. The lion hunt of King Ashurnasirpal (884-859 BC). Courtesy, Trustees of the British Museum.

Figure 32. The celebrated Black Obelisk of Shalmaneser III (860-824 BC). Courtesy, Trustees of the British Museum.

Pergamum and Attalia; Smyrna, Ephesus and Miletus. Those of the Dorians who did not stay in the land and the cities they had conquered in the Peloponnesus, continued their depredations across the Aegean, settling at last in Lycia, in the south-western corner of Asia Minor once part of the Luwian state, The majority made the Peloponnesus their home. Homer's *Iliad* describes a war (the Trojan war) in a minute corner of the great landscape whose character was changed by the fierce "Sea and Land Peoples" who descended like locusts upon the greatness and wealth of regulated and established civilizations.

The consequences were immense: Assyria arose as the dominant power over ancient states whose strength had either been sapped or destroyed; and over newcomers who possessed neither experience, power nor stability. In western Anatolia Phrygia became the heir of the Hittite kingdom and remained a dominant power, under its Midas kings, for 500 years. The southern rump of Khatti gathered itself together, with Karchemish as its centre, and eventually became a considerable kingdom – the Biblical Hittites (Jud.I.26). It controlled the crossing of the Euphrates and extended northward as far as Adana, in eastern Cilicia. In central and eastern Anatolia arose the pre-Armenian, Hurrian kingdom of Urartu, which was to frustrate Assyria in her Anatolian ambitions for 600 years, right up to the death of Assyria herself, in 607 BC. In the south, after the end of the Kassite dynasty (1156), Babylonia lived in constant fear of her aggressive northern neighbour, Assyria – a perpetual threat. In the west, Syria, with its great ports of Ugarit, Byblos, Poeseideïon, recovered its mercantile importance, much as the Phoenician ports of Sidon and Tyre. The Jewish kingdom of Israel was established by Joshua, and the Philistines with their iron weapons, were eventually driven out when the secret of smelting iron ore became common knowledge.

The movements of peoples continued on the fringes of the new political configuration: In the east there appeared new settlements of Aryan peoples, especially the Medes and the Parsua (the latter, perhaps the predecessors of the Persians) first mentioned in the annals of Assyria's king Shalmaneser III (859-824), who made settlements to the south of Lake Urmia, in the vicinity of the non-Aryan, but historically important, indigenous Manaeans (the Biblical 'Minni' (Jer. 51. 27.)).

Early in the eighth century, the appearance, from the north, of the Scythian and Kimmerian horsemen in Anatolia for the first time, is reported by Herodotus (IV.12). 'This may well be the result of the very impulse given by the Chinese when they drove out the Huns, c. 800 BC, recorded by Greeks, Hebrews and Assyrians.'[5] The Kimmerians attacked Urartu and Phrygia. But, later, Lydia destroyed the Kimmerians (c. 620). The Scythians became involved as allies of the Medes and the neo-Babylonian empire against Assyria, which they together annihilated (c. 607).

Notes

1. Barnett, 'The Sea Peoples', CAH II², p. 369.
2. Barnett R.D., 'Phrygia and the Peoples of Anatolia in the Iron Age', CAH II². p. 418.
3. Barnett R.D., *ibid.* pp. 361, 418.
4. Sanders N.K., *The Sea Peoples*, Thames & Hudson, London, 1978.
5. Minns E.H., 'The Scythians and Northern Nomads', CAH III, ch. IX, p. 188

Chapter 9
Assyria

The situation down to the end of the last chapter might be briefly restated: (1) From Neolithic beginnings, through a period of pottery cultures, particularly those of Halaf and 'Ubaid, we reached the high Sumerian, literate civilization, with a cuneiform script, which was adopted throughout the Near East – except Egypt, which invented its own hieroglyphic writing with affinities to that of Sumerian,[1] used down to the first century BC; (2) a surge of Semitic peoples out of Arabia, infiltrated Sumero-Babylonian territories, and eventually (c.2400) established the kingdom of Akkad-Babylon, which reached its apogee under Sargon of Akkad and his grandson Naram-Sin. They ruled an empire reaching from Sumer-Akkad to the Mediterranean in the north-west and Elam in the south-east – the Babylonian Empire; (3) Hammurabi, of the Babylonian dynasty, frustrated the ambitions of the first king of Assyria, Shamshi-Adad (1813-1781), by seizing his capital, Ashur and its main tributary, Mari, and himself reaching out to the great ports of the Mediterranean (c.1770). He is remembered as a powerful ruler and especially for codifying and making additions to the ancient laws of Sumer-Akkad; (4) Hammurabi's weak successors (down to c.1595) were unable to sustain Babylonian rule over such a huge empire, particularly as by that time Anatolia and north Mesopotamia had been overrun by Aryan newcomers – the Hittites and the aristocratic horse-riding Mitanni; (5) the Jews were among the Semitic peoples who had overrun Sumer, Abraham's tribe with them. Abraham (c.1850) and his tribe travelled from Ur to Harran and so to Palestine, adopting *en route*, some of the legends of Babylonia which have been transmitted to us in the Old Testament; (6) a diversion must be made here, from Mesopotamia to Egypt. Seemingly, Sumerian immigrants markedly influenced the development of Egyptian hieroglyphics[2] and other aspects of Egyptian society and politics, which produced an empire reaching down from the Delta to the First Cataract, and beyond; (7) the Cretan or Minoan civilization is inextricably associated with the Mycenaeans; both peoples were powerful thalassocracies, with strong trading interests in the Levant and Anatolia; but the Mycenaeans are connected with Homer's Achaeans or *Achaeoi* who are equated by an increasing number of scholars with the powerful kingdom of Ahhiyawa (after c.1350), in north-western Anatolia.

Figure 33. Ivory plaque with griffin-headed guardian figure. Excavated near Van, Eastern Turkey, Urartian c. 700 BC, ht 9.8cm. Courtesy, Trustees of the British Museum.

These events took place before the end of the thirteenth century. By that time Crete had been partially destroyed by a great earthquake and, around 1450,, invaded by Mycenaeans; Babylonia had been appropriated by an Aryan people, the Kassites (c.1570-c.1160); Mitanni had been destroyed by Assyria (1275), and Egypt and Khatti had come to terms in the face of a growing Assyrian threat (1269); by c.1200, the Hittite Empire had been overrun by the Phrygians. A much reduced neo-Hittite kingdom continued to flourish with its centre at Carchemish, in northern Syria.

After the immense changes wrought by the invasions of the Sea and Land Peoples, over a period of 100 years, around the end of the thirteenth century, Assyria arose from the ashes of the defunct ancient kingdoms as the new political power which was to dominate and ruthlessly exploit its might from the Zagros mountains to the Levant for 600 years.

Shalmaneser I (1275-1245) destroyed Mitanni (1275) and invaded northern Syria (Khanigalbat). At the same time he totally defeated the Hittite king, slaughtering his army 'like sheep'. But he suffered a setback in a battle against the new Hurrian kingdom of Urartu in Armenia (1275) which had probably been

Figure 34. Tiglath-Pileser III, King of Assyria (744-727 BC) in triumph. Stone bas-relief from Nimrud (Calah). Courtesy, Trustees of the British Museum.

reinforced and reorganised by its neighbouring cousins, the fugitive Hurrian-Mitannian king and his aristocracy. A fusion of Hurrian tribes living in the Armenian highlands resulted over a period of time in the rise of the powerful kingdom of Ararat (or Urartu) with its heartlands in the region round Lake Van. It was to be a constant thorn in Assyria's body-politic until the end of its days (607).

From c.1240, Assyria became the leading military power in the Near East: Shalmaneser's son, Tukulti-Ninurta (1245-1208), successfully subdued the Hurrian chieftainships of the upper Tigris, such as Alzi, Purukuzzi, Amadani (modern Diarbekir district), to which he refers collectively as the land of Shubari, where he boasts of having sacked 180 towns. His inroads into the mountainous regions of that 'foreign' land were, incidentally, exploratory. He found himself in 'pathless, mighty mountains', with 'untrodden paths' which he 'broadened with my bronze axes' for the passage of his army and chariot regiments. He claims to have reached the 'Upper Sea' (perhaps Lake Van). Many kings of the Nairi or Riverlands were taken prisoner and with copper chains round their necks, taken to his capital, Ashur. The Shubari lands gave to Assyria control of the routes leading across the Euphrates and (river) Murad su into central and eastern Anatolia and its mineral riches (especially the valuable copper mines) as well as cattle and, particularly, the fine horses of the region. Although he calls himself 'King of the Nairi lands', in fact neither he nor any of his successors ever subjugated those hardy mountain peoples for any significant length of time. The result of that, and successive, Assyrian forays into the Riverlands was to encourage the federation of the racially related inhabitants, under Urartian leadership.

Tukulti-Ninurta also overran Kassite Babylonia. He occupied the whole country, from the middle and northern Euphrates, including the important city of Mari and that of Arapkha, at the end of the trade route from Iran down to the Persian Gulf. His inscription boasts:

> Trusting in the great gods, my lords, and Ishtar, the queen of heaven and earth, who went at the head of my army, I forced Kashtiliash (Kassite King of Babylon, 1242-1235) to join battle with me.

The Babylonians were defeated and their king taken prisoner.

Figure 35. Ashurbanipal killing a wounded lion. From the palace of Ashurbanipal at Nineveh, c. 645 BC. Courtesy, Trustees of the British Museum.

My foot trod upon his royal neck. He was to me as a foot-stool. I brought him, captive, stripped and bound, before the god, Ashur my lord. All Sumer and Akkad I forced under my sway, even down to the Lower Sea of the rising sun.

Babylon's city walls were dismantled, Marduk's temple was plundered, the inhabitants were slaughtered and the city given to the torch (1235). Babylon was a transit stage of caravans travelling between east and west, as well as an ancient centre of culture which Assyria had always respected and coveted. It was therefore an important source of income for the treasury as well as a source of knowledge. Besides the loot of Marduk's temple, the Assyrian king carried away large quantities of Babylonian cuneiform tablets.[3] This is how Assyrian victories were celebrated and the king's arrogance assuaged. Kashtiliash's three successors were minor, vassal kings of Kassite-Babylon, paying tribute to Assyria. Kassite subjection lasted seven years, down to 1228. Then a successful revolt restored the Kassite dynasty. A Babylonian chronicle records: 'The nobles of Akkad and Karduniash (the Kassite name for Babylonia) revolted, and they sat Adad-shum-usur on the throne of his father.' (1219-1180)[4]

Twenty-five years after the defeat of Kashtiliash (1210), the peoples of the Nairi and the Zagros mountains successfully rebelled. Then the Neo-Hittite kingdom (with Karchemish as its centre) defeated Tukulti-Ninurta, (1245-1208) when he attempted to retain his gains in northern Syria. Weakened by successive misfortunes, he became the victim of a palace revolution. The conspirators tore him from his throne and

In Kar-Tukulti-Ninurta (the king's palace in his new capital on the Tigris, opposite Ashur) in a house they shut him up and slew him with the sword (1208).

Kassite-Babylon was not humiliated by Assyrian arms alone. It had also suffered sporadic attacks and invasions by the powerful kings of Elam in the south-east. After 1161, it was subjected either to Elamite or Assyrian attacks. Elam, rather than Assyria, seems to have been the more ferocious enemy – the mind boggles at such a concept. The dogged Kassite resistance was of no avail; their tablets inform us that in 1160 a vast army led by the Elamite usurper, whose

crimes were greater and his grievous sins worse than all his fathers had

committed . . . like a deluge he laid low all the peoples of Akkad and cast in
ruins Babylon and the noblest cities of sanctity.[5]

In 1157, after a fierce struggle with Elam, the last Kassite king was defeated and
captured; the stele of the god Marduk was seized and carried away – the ultimate
humiliation, indeed death, of the nation – and Babylon was occupied. Among
other treasure, they carried away Hammurabi's celebrated table of laws, as well
as the great stele of Naram-Sin and the Obelisk of Manishtusu to Susa, the Elamite
capital. The Kassite-Babylonian kingdom disintegrated; and so ended the long
dynasty of the Kassite kings in the history of Babylon. Starting as mere nomad
chieftains, they had seized an established and respected kingdom and managed
to reign creditably for almost 600 years, down to 1157. The Kassites had

ruled a unified Babylonia far longer than any other Mesopotamian dynasty,
and the emergence of Babylon as the political and cultural centre of the ancient
world took place under their aegis.[6]

The date 1157 and the events preceding it in Babylonia, coincided with the great
movements of the Sea and Land Peoples and the immense political changes
described in chapter 8.

A long phase of political instability followed the end of the Kassite dynasty
(1157). Thenceforth, down to the eighth century, the country was ruled by a
number of true Babylonian royal dynasties, the only period in the history of
Babylon when native Babylonians were dominant. The first of these dynasties
was associated with the city of Isin (the Second Dynasty of Isin, or the Fourth
Dynasty of Babylon), where native resistance to the Elamites had culminated in
the rise of the first Babylonian king with the celebrated name of Nebuchadnezzar
I (1127-1105). He determined to avenge the savage Elamite sack of Babylon.
His initial assault on Elam became an unmitigated disaster when a plague
overwhelmed his troops and he himself nearly lost his life in the turmoil of flight.
The king's second attempt was successful and his exploits are inscribed on a
stele which describes his painful, but determined march across desert country
to the Elamite capital, Susa, in a temperature of perhaps 50°C.

From Dêr, the holy city of Anu, he (the King of Babylon) made a leap of
thirty double leagues. In the month of Tamuz (July-August) he took the road.
The blades of the picks burn like fire; the stones of the track blaze like
furnaces; there is no water (in the wadis) and the walls are dry; stop the
strongest of the horses and stagger the young heroes. Yet he goes, the elected

*Figure 36. The dying
lioness. Detail from
Ashurbanipal's lion
hunt series of stone bas-
reliefs. From Nineveh,
c. 645 BC. Courtesy,
Trustees of the British
Museum.*

king supported by the gods; he marches on, Nebuchadnezzar who has no rival.[7]

Such descriptions represent a decisive victory and songs of elation. The battle was fought and won on the banks of the river Karun. The king of Elam fled and no more is heard of him. Nebuchadnezzar took Elam in triumph and plundered its treasures. It was some years before Elam recovered from that military disaster. Babylonian self-respect was restored.

Of special importance was the return of Marduk's effigy from Susa to Babylon, for unlike the Egyptian pharaohs who were worshipped as the reincarnation of god, the Near Eastern kings were only his representatives. Marduk's prestige had been rising significantly during the period of the statue's 'exile'; his cult had spread, and even Assyria had adopted him. But it was only after his return to Babylon that Marduk's glory of a supreme deity was restored. The victory of the Babylonian king gave him a place among the ancient heroes, and his deeds were inscribed and recited by successive generations.

Sumer and Ur, in spite of so many political vicissitudes, remained as centres of respect and piety, for, not only Marduk, but the early deities of Sumer, too, were remembered by Nebuchadnezzar. Objects of gold and silver, and a stele inscribed with her duties and rituals in her ceremonial dress, are dedicated to the priestess of the moon-god. That votive offering indicates the possibility that Nebuchadnezzar, in accordance with the customs of ancient Akkad and the Old Babylonian kings, had installed his own daughter as high priestess at Ur. After Nebuchadnezzar (1105), Babylonia went into a serious decline.

Only forty years after the destruction of the Babylonian-Kassite dynasty (1157) the great name of Tiglath-Pileser I (1115-1077) appears on the Assyrian king lists. To the north-west, in Anatolia, for some fifty years, the rich valleys of Alzi and Purukuzzi had been occupied by the Mushki, always associated by the Assyrians with Phrygia, although the original Mushki home-lands were in the area of the Chalybes. A horde of 20,000 came down the Tigris valley, dominating the countryside west of the Upper Tigris, threatening Nineveh and fomenting revolt, and was defeated by Tiglath-Pileser. A year later he won back Subartu and the districts east of Tigris, along the river Zab.

Having broken the power of the Mushki and their allies, the Assyrian king could turn his attention to the Nairi riverlands, north-west of Lake Van. A decisive battle was fought in which a coalition of twenty three Nairi chiefs was defeated. Another encounter took place against the forces of Milid (Malatya) the most ancient homelands of the Armenians[8] who were forced to pay tribute in lead-lumps. On these hill-frontiers especially, the naturally independent, spirited peoples would henceforth be forced to group into large defensive units. Thus, Assyrian fortunes prospered, especially under Tiglath-Pileser I. He celebrated his successes by building a new capital for himself at Kalhu (the Biblical Calah, Gen.X.11).

Tiglath-Pileser's successor, Ashur-bel-kala (1074-1057), drove invading Syrio-Aramaeans out of 'Uruatri' (Urartu) and himself crossed the Euphrates into Syria and so to the Mediterranean coastlands. Later, a relief designed by order of King Adad-nirari II (911-899), on what is now known as the 'Broken

Obelisk', from Nineveh, shows a king '(perhaps Tiglath-Pileser I) holding in one hand a cord made fast to the nostrils of four suppliant prisoners: above him are the symbols of the five chief gods; from the sun's disc a hand comes out presenting a bow and arrows to the king.[9]

During one hundred years of relatively weak Assyrian kings in the eleventh century, and a period of inactivity at the same time in Egypt and Babylon, the Middle Land (Syria-Palestine) was free. The three newcomers in that free land were the Philistines and the Israelites in the south, and the Aramaeans in the north. The Israelites and Aramaeans invaded the territories of the Canaanites and Amorites and, in the course of time absorbed its inhabitants. The Philistines could not achieve this; they had no allies; they were not Semites, but uncircumcised foreigners from the Aegean, perhaps from Crete, who could not possibly fraternise with Semites, particularly as the Jewish and Aramaean invasions preceded theirs. Eventually, they were destroyed or expelled. But the Semitic Phoenicians, who could retire, if necessary, to their insulated, sea-girt fortress of Tyre and the safety of their ships, were immune from any Israelite, Aramaean or Philistine threat. They sailed further and ever further westwards trading with and colonising many Mediterranean ports, and diffusing the ancient Near Eastern cultural achievements. Among other Phoenician colonies Gades (Spain-Gibraltar), Tarshish (Tartessus in Spain),[10] also Carthage and Utica (just west of Carthage) must be mentioned. Carthage, the greatest colony of them all, was founded towards the end of the ninth century, a little after the time of King Ahab of Israel (874-853). Utica, Gades and Tarshish were much older, Tarshish having been a trading station since Solomon.

The others in Palestine, the conquerors and the conquered, marched up and down the coast, with its backdrop of mountains, battering one another and fatefully awaiting the arrival of their destinies at the hands of outside conquerors – the Assyrians, the Babylonians, the Medes, and the Persians.

At this point of Assyrian weakness and before its resurgence as a great military power, the question of transport might be briefly introduced. How did huge armies, with their considerable equipment, travel over the length and breadth of the extensive empire? They must have continued to expand the network of rough, 'straightened' pathways initiated by the Sumerians and continued by the Babylonians. But, strangely, the question of road engineering on a large, permanent scale does not seem to have occurred to the Mesopotamian rulers. Within the cities and outside its walls, leading to religious sites or to mines and quarries, roads were indeed carefully laid and paved, so that heavily laden waggons could more easily travel. But, beyond that, records inform us of military carts, waggons and chariots being bogged down in muddy paths and soldiers having to unload and reload waggons, chariots being manhandled over mountains, and, in the absence of bridges over rivers, fording them where possible, or crossing them on rafts. At first the donkey and onager were used as beasts of burden and for hauling heavy waggons and carts. Although horse-riding invaders from India (Mitannians) and Central Asia (Medes and Persians) overran the mountainous regions to the east of Mesopotamia, in spite of the increasing use of the horse after the thirteenth century, Assyria seems to have been unaware of its use as an adept and swift animal for drawing war-chariots and for mounted soldiery, until the ninth century. The most important part of Anatolian tribute for Tukulti-Ninurta II (889-884), was that of horses for the king's bodyguard. It was about this time that regiments of chariots with wheels of six spokes (rather than four, as in Egypt) seem to have been introduced into the Assyrian forces.[11]

Their knowledge of breaking in and training horses for the king's messengers, for the development of a cavalry, as well as for team work, harnessing them for chariot warfare and other purposes, owed much to a Hurri-Mitannian text on those skills, discovered in modern times.[12]

A disorganised political situation in Mesopotamia, due to Aramaean incursion, was seized by Assyria to revive its own fortunes. A new dynasty was founded by Ashur-rabi II (1013-973). His work of restoration was continued by his successors, and evidence of success and power are demonstrated in the extravagant building activities of the kings down to the end of the tenth century. These expensive reconstructions and new buildings were expressions of the triumphant military adventures which restored Assyrian prestige. Adad-nirari I (911-890) traversed the territories to the south-east and reasserted Assyrian supremacy in the lands south of the Lower Zab down to the northern frontiers of Elam, and beyond as far as the southern edge of modern Persia. He also subdued a king of the eighth dynasty of Babylon by the capture of the strategically important Babylonian city of Arapkha (Karkar).[13]

Shalmaneser III (858-824) invaded Israel, destroyed the fortress city of Hazor, reached Mount Carmel and turned north into Phoenicia. Jehu, King of Israel, paid him tribute (841). In the 1840's, among the ruins of Nineveh, one of the first exciting finds by Henry Layard was the famous Black Obelisk, now on display at the British Museum. Carved upon it, Jehu is seen on his knees in an attitude of prayer before his conqueror. Israel is there described as 'Land of the House of Omri', and Jehu, the usurper, as 'son of Omri'. In the later part of the ninth century, while Assyria was preoccupied by wars with its great northern rival, Urartu (which dominated central and eastern Anatolia, parts of Mesopotamia and northern Syria), Israel and Judaea enjoyed a period of relative freedom from external threats, although there was constant warfare within.

The political scene changed dramatically with the ascension of the Biblical King Pul (2 Kings 15), to the throne of Assyria, the historical Tiglath-Pileser III (744-727). He broke the power of Urartu (see below) in Syria and Mesopotamia, and crushed Israel, taking captive many of its leaders. Then the fury of his successor, Sargon II (722-705) destroyed Israel; and his son, Sennacherib (705-681), subdued Judaea. The latter's campaign in Palestine is famous for the successful siege and capture of Lachish, and the siege of Jerusalem, when King Hezekiel built a tunnel through the city walls to supply water to his defenders and citizens (2 Kings XX.20). During the course of that great war in Judaea forty six cities fell before the Assyrians, the most important of which was Lachish (701); and Judaea paid tribute to Assyria, until Babylonia's Nebuchadnezzar II (604-562) destroyed Lachish and took the Judaeans into captivity to Babylon.

Babylon, itself, seems to have survived Assyrian rampages in Mesopotamia and elsewhere, due, it seems, to Babylonian diplomacy and to some extent, to

Assyrian respect for its cultural inheritance. In the ninth century there were exchanges of royal brides, and when Assyrian monarchs trespassed on Babylonian territory, in their hunting excursions or whatever other reason, the Babylonians diplomatically acquiesced.

Ninth century Babylonia appears to have been particularly prosperous. Cultural activities, especially in literature, also flourished. A treaty with Assyria's Shalmaneser III assured its safety from internal conspirators against the throne, as well as from external threats. Such was the friendship between the allies that

> Shalmaneser personally visited the principal cult centres, offered sacrifices, presented lavish gifts and endowments, fêted the citizens of Babylon and Borsippa, 'gave them food and wine, clothed them in brightly coloured garments and presented them with gifts', hardly an Assyrian king's usual behaviour towards subject peoples, and once again evidence of the cultural dominance exercised by Babylon upon its northern neighbour.[14]

This was in marked contrast to Assyria's ravages into the south-west against Chaldea, a region peopled by Semitic tribes, tent dwellers and robbers, but proving themselves to be of an independent spirit and belligerent, unlike the more northern Babylonians, who preferred peace with Assyria to unqualified political freedom. (It may not be irrelevant to comment that 'tent dwellers' are described as 'robbers' whereas city dwellers who invade and appropriate that which is not theirs are described as 'conquerors'). In short it is almost true to say that for about four centuries, until the demise of Assyria itself (ironically at the hands of Babylon), Babylon existed by courtesy of Assyria.

For example, on the accession to the Assyrian throne of Shalmaneser's successor, Shamshi-Adad V (823-811), a revolt broke out which spread throughout the kingdom. Babylon went to Assyria's assistance. This was a way of repaying a debt to Assyria for its support of Babylon in the past. But, after the successful suppression of the revolution, the Babylonians presented Assyria with a humiliating treaty. Shamshi-Adad soon showed his southern neighbours how much they had erred in their judgement. Two successive Babylonian kings were carried off as prisoners to Assyria, and anarchy prevailed in Babylonia. Then:

> 13,000 of their warriors I cut down with the sword. Their blood like the waters of a stream I caused to run through the squares of their city. The corpses of their soldiers I piled in heaps . . . . His [the Babylonian king's] royal bed, his royal couch, the treasure of his palaces, his property, his gods and everything from his palace, without number, I carried away. His captive warriors were given to the soldiers of my land like grasshoppers. The city [Dur-Papsukal, an island fortress to which the Babylonian army had fled] I destroyed, I devastated, I burnt with fire and "Shamshi-Adad laid claim to the whole of the country under the ancient title of 'King of Sumer and Akkad.[15]

On the death of Shamshi-Adad, his queen, Shammu-ramat, the Semiramis of Greek legend, ruled as regent for five years for her young son, Adad-Nirari III (811-783). She was a powerful lady who made dedications in her own name, placing them before those of her son. Her true or legendary adventures are told by Diodorus of Sicily. In Armenian folklore she is associated with the Armenian legendary king Ara, the Fair, with whom she was enamoured. Unfortunately, his response was cool. Furious, and her pride wounded, she went to war against him.

In spite of strict instructions to her soldiery not to kill him, a chance arrow fatally struck down her hero. This legend is told by the Armenian historian Moses of Khoren (who flourished early in the Middle Ages). He indicates as the source of his tale, the inscriptions on the rock-face of the fortress of Van, which led a French scholar and a German archaeologist (financed by the French) to an investigation which revealed the existence of the pre-Armenian (pre-600 BC) civilization of Urartu.

In the south-east, Elam, which supported the Chaldeans, had always been, and remained, a defiant enemy of Assyria, until it was destroyed by Ashurbanipal in the seventh century. But Assyria was to regret that for she was to bear the historical burden of her own extermination in consequence. Elam had been a powerful buffer state between the aggressive Aryan Medes and Persians in the east and the ancient civilizations of Babylonia and Assyria in Mesopotamia.

THE KINGDOM OF URARTU: For almost a century after the reign of Shalmaneser III, the northern kingdom of Urartu (Assyrian) or Ararat (Hebrew) grew apace in power and by the time of Adad-Nirari III's reign (811-782) its kings ruled an empire which threatened the very existence of Assyria. It is, therefore, desirable to outline briefly the history of that pre-Armenian civilization, which, in the sense of historical sequence, could be comparable to Gaul-France. The culture and civilization of Urartu must have been dominant all over the area that we now know as eastern Turkey, Caucasia and north Persia and it has been suggested that one must look for the origins of much of (Persian) Achaemenid art, architecture and even state protocol and writing in Urartu.[16]

As early as the seventeenth or sixteenth century BC the Babylonians knew of the Armenian highlands as the land of *Urdhu* (possibly the contracted form of *Urardhu)*. It is also found in the *Qumrum* 'Dead Sea' texts as (H)urartu.[17] The people who had settled there since c.2400 were Hurrians (as were the later settlers in northern Mesopotamia whose rulers were the aristocratic Mitanni). They seem to have been strongly Armenoid in physical type.[18]

The Armenian highlands, loosely inhabited by those Urartian clans or tribes, appear to have been organised into increasingly larger units, until they were powerful enough to defy their fearful southern neighbour, Assyria. Shalmaneser I mentions them first in 1275 when there was a successful Urartian attack against Assyrian forces. The year 1275 coincides with the defeat and annihilation of the Mitannians, by Assyria. Their king and aristocracy escaped. Where did they escape to? The most obvious place appears to be the land of their Hurrian cousins, the neighbouring Urartians, adjoining their north-eastern frontiers. It is not difficult to surmise that the Urartian victory over Shalmaneser could have been due to a large extent to Mitannian experienced leadership.

No more is heard of Urartu until the appearance of its first known king, Aramu (as he is called in Assyrian documents) or Aram, in Armenian tradition (c.858-844). He was able to withstand Shalmaneser III's incursions into his territories and ultimately to force him to withdraw. Aramu's successor, Sarduri I (844-828) established a new dynasty, which was to last to the end of his country's history in c.590. He built what proved to be an impregnable fortress and, around it, his capital city of Tushpa, on the east coast of Lake Van. He knitted together the various Urartian chieftainships into a unified kingdom, so that his successor, King Ishpuini, the Establisher, who ruled concurrently with his son, Menua, was able to expand, and to gain the respect of neighbouring peoples. After his father's death in 810 Menua formed 'The Federation of the North', consisting of Hurrian principalities. Urartian rule and influence then reached from the Caspian in the east and the small, but important buffer state of Musasir in the south-east, to the north-south bend of the river Euphrates in the west, and so to Hamath and Alalakh on the Orontes, giving access to the Mediterranean at the port of Poseideïon (al-Mina). He died in 785, having brought his father's work to fruition and established a powerful kingdom to the north of Assyria.

He was followed by Argishti I (785-753), and Sarduri II (753-735) who actually ruled an empire which included the Assyrian homelands to the very gates of Nineveh, and the river Dyala marked the south-eastern boundaries of the empire. The port of Poseideïon, at the mouth of the river Orontes, was occupied and used as an outlet for the famous Urartian bronzes, particularly ceremonial cauldrons with artistic handle-mounts, which were shipped even as far as Etruria in Italy. The caravans from India, China and Media then passed through Urartian territory to the Black Sea and Mediterranean ports, bringing wealth and prestige to that country. The Black Sea ports were occupied by Greek colonists. The Milesian Trapezus was founded in c.754. But the Greeks did not go as far as the eastern tip of the Black Sea where Colchis (Qulhi) was taken and occupied by Sarduri II. It is, therefore, probable that an Urartian port was to be found there, although no archaeological evidence of such a port has yet come to light.

It was Tiglath-Pileser III (745-727), who reorganised the army and the administration of Assyria. He expelled Urartu from Mesopotamia and northern Syria and saved his country. His successor, the powerful Sargon II (722-705) destroyed Israel, and subdued Hittite Karchemish. In his successful campaign against Urartu (713), via its eastern frontiers, he laid low a cluster of small Aryan states as well as the aboriginal Mannai (the Minni of the Bible Jer.LI.27), allies of Urartu. He was supreme over the whole of western Asia, except for Urartu which although defeated, had not been occupied. However, he had not reckoned with the wild Kimmerian tribes which had crossed the Caucasus. They had been confronted and diverted westwards by Urartu, just when Sargon was attacking her in the south-east – a reason for the Urartian defeat. The Kimmerians subsequently clashed with the Phrygian forces in the west, causing King Midas (of the 'Golden Touch') to commit suicide. However, south of Tabal, at a decisive battle with Assyria, they were defeated and dispersed. But King Sargon was killed in that battle (705).

Sennacherib (705-681) succeeded Sargon and took control of his empire. He besieged Lachish in Palestine and destroyed Jerusalem. News of a plot to depose him caused him to return to his capital, Nineveh, where he was murdered by his two sons, Adramelech and Sharezer, as told in the Old Testament, 'while he was praying in the House of Nisroch, his god . . . and they fled into the land of Armenia.' (2 Kings XIX.37).

A brief diversion must be made here to ask: Where was that Biblical 'land of Armenia' situated? It must have included the whole of what is now central and eastern Turkey, the site of Urartu or Ararat. Thus, Noah's Ark came to rest 'on the Mountains [of the kingdom] of Ararat' (Gen.VIII.4), not on Mount Ararat Having regard to the date of Sennacherib's death (681), the one province 'in the land of Armenia' to which the patricides could have escaped, without going into enemy territory of Urartu, would have been Shupria, west of Lake Van, in the upper reaches of the river Tigris, at that time an independent state, owing allegiance neither to Urartu nor to Assyria. It occupied, approximately, the region of the later Sophene.

In the chapter on the Sea Peoples, reference was made to the Phrygians, who took part in the invasion and destruction of the Hittite Empire. It seems that an Armenian tribe, within the Phrygian horde, was in the vanguard. Herodotus (VII.73) writes that the Armenians were Phrygian colonists (from Thessaly); Strabo (XI,13.10, XI.14.12) describes them as wearing the Thessalian costume, thus supporting Herodotus. He also writes (XI.iv.7) that 'Armenos, the Thessalian, was Jason's companion on his expedition of discovery to the Colchi', and beyond. Eudoxus of Cnidus, (quoted by Stephanos of Byzantium, *Ethnica*) adds that there were similarities between the languages of the Phrygians and the Armenians. But modern scholars, while not entirely rejecting the Greek writers, show that Armenians were probably mainly an indigenous people of Asia Minor[19] who intermarried with the Urartians and the Armeno-Phrygians. 'The one remaining major Indo-European language which constitutes a branch of the family in itself (as does Greek) is Armenian.'[20]

The Armeno-Phrygians then, having witnessed and probably taken part in the destruction of Khatti, infiltrated the Hurrian provinces of Urartu. It is quite possible, in these circumstances, that a large section of them seized the mountainous province of Shupria, perhaps in the twelfth or eleventh century, and by the eighth century, had established an Armenian chieftainship or kingdom of the whole or part of Shupria.[21]

The events which followed the assassination of King Sennacherib of Assyria, are concerned with the ambition of his third son, Esarhaddon (681-668) – the conquest of Egypt. But, before attempting that major campaign, he had to put an end to the palace revolution which had cost his father's life, and to face an invasion of Kimmerians in 678 under their chief, Teushpa who having ravaged the Phrygian kingdom of Midas, had overrun almost the whole of western Asia Minor. They had been a great power for over thirty years. In 676 Esarhaddon had to repel a much more dangerous eruption of Scythians, another Aryan tribe, from the east. Victorious, he diplomatically gave his daughter in marriage to Bartatua, the Scythian chief (the Protothyes of Herodotus I.103). A romantic tradition has it that the Assyrian princess's dowry consisted of the fabulous treasure of Ziwiye (Persian Kurdistan), a hoard of fine gold objects of different artistic styles of the period c.700 BC, found in a metal tub in 1947, and now exhibited at the British Museum. He went on to put down revolts in Sidon and Phoenicia (677-671). Only then was he ready for his overwhelming assault on the Egyptian (Nubian) XXVth Dynasty. In four months he conquered the entire Delta and seized Memphis. However, Egypt's gods must have been against him, for he fell ill during the campaign and died two years later.

Figure 37. The Ziwiye Treasure, seventh century BC. Gold pectoral ornament, gold eagle or griffin head (Urartian) and a sheet of gold with a pattern of alternating stags and ibexes. Courtesy, Trustees of the British Museum.

Esarhaddon's work was completed by his son, Ashurbanipal (668-624) who subjugated the whole of Egypt. In 648 he turned his frightful attention to Elam, which had defied all comers for 2000 years. He ravaged and destroyed it systematically, even sowing the land with salt in order to render it infertile, as his forebear, Sargon II, had done in Urartu 100 years earlier. That deadly work was crowned in c. 640 by the sacking of the capital, Susa. At that time Ashurbanipal was indeed 'Lord of the World', as it was then known. All except for Anatolia and Urartu, Assyria's ancient Armenian rival. These remained independent, and ambassadors of the two countries resided in their respective capitals. They seem to have realised the advisability of forgetting old rivalries in the face of widespread Kimmerian invasions in the west, and Scythians in the east.

In that warrior nation of Assyria the army and the king played the essential rôle. The sovereign was the source of all authority. As the representative of the gods, he was above mere mortals and lived in his palace apart from them, isolated in his majesty. As in Sumer and down to the end of Assyria's turbulent history, wars were waged and, at the same time, great works were undertaken in the name of the chief god, 'Ashur, my lord', whose effigy was sacrosanct, as Marduk's was in Babylon, Enlil's in Sumer and Khaldi's in Urartu. It was the desire of every Assyrian king to erect his own palace, if not to build an entirely new capital city. Thus, Shalmaneser I (1275-1245) founded Kalhu, Ashur-dan II (933-912), Nineveh and Sargon II (722-705) founded Dur-Sharrukin (Khorsabad). The king's primary function was to command the army, which was largely composed of mercenary troops under Assyrian officers, and its effectiveness in battle much depended on its heavy chariots. It was, however, no less invincible in the art of the siege, and its corps of sappers and engineers was furnished with a variety of sophisticated siege equipment.

The civil administration is not so well documented and appears to have been less skilfully organised. Nevertheless, that department continued to expand, and during the reign of Ashurbanipal, authority almost everywhere was in the hands of governors, assisted by scribes whose frequent and detailed reports kept the king well informed of everything, including any subversive movements which might disturb the security of the empire.

LYDIA: Lydia (with Greek pretensions) was one of the earliest kingdoms in western Anatolia. At first unmolested by any other power, Lydia was able to achieve stability and wealth. Its history is closely related to the Greek Ionian states, which exerted an indispensable influence on Greece. However, it was briefly an important power in the seventh century, when it had diplomatic relations with Ashurbanipal of Assyria. It destroyed the remnants of Phrygia dispersing for ever the Kimmerians, and under its king Alyattes (c.617-558), successfully confronted the powerful Median forces. The Lydian invention of coined money (probably inspired by eighth century Assyrian examples) was adopted by Ionia and the neighbouring Aegean islands. They were primitive electrum (a mixture of gold and silver) pieces; those struck by Croesus in the sixth century bore the royal effigy. The earliest royal houses have mythical antecedents. The first of the historical kings was Gyges ('Gugu') who after an intrigue with the queen and the murder of king Candaulus of the House of Heraclid (Herod.I.4, 5-7), founded the royal house of the Mermnad dynasty ('House of the Hawk'). Gyges' origin is a matter of scholarly discussion. Some offer the view that he was the first true Lydian to gain power, c.685.[22]

Gyges found himself threatened by a northern horde of Gimirrai or Kimmerians (who had already destroyed Phrygia). He begged Assyria's king Ashurbanipal for help:

and obtained a sufficient material assistance to defeat the northerners and send two of their chiefs in chains to Nineveh. A little later, in 660, we find him and his people definitely enrolled among the feudatories of Ashurbanipal. But Lydia joined Egypt in an uprising against Assyria. The Kimmerians then, led by their chieftain, Tugdame (Strabo's Lygdamis) took advantage of Gyges' preoccupation in that adventure: they attacked and defeated the Lydian forces. Gyges was killed in that battle (c.652).[23]

His son, Ardys (678-629), appears to have come to terms with Ashurbanipal, and finally, aided by Ionians whose cities had been sacked by the Kimmerians, he drove them and their leader, Tugdamme, out of Western Asia Minor. At the Cilician Gates they were met and defeated by the Assyrians (c.637). Tugdamme was killed, and the horde retreated northwards, where it was probably destroyed by Madyes, the Scyth.[24] The successors of Ardys were Sadyattes and Alyattes. Alyattes (617-560) was unencumbered either by Kimmerians or Assyrians. For Ashurbanipal had died in 624, having ruled over his country's greatest ever territorial extent. Moreover, during his reign, Assyria had reached the zenith of its civilization.

Thus, Alyattes was able to expand his kingdom eastwards, as far as the river Halys and westwards to the Mediterranean, capturing the important city of Smyrna. He secured the friendship of Ephesus by marrying his daughter to its dictator, Melas. The ancient city of Miletus was more difficult to conciliate. He succeeded in doing so, however, by presenting golden gifts to the oracle of Delphi, thus not only retaining the friendship of Miletus, but also insinuating himself and Lydia into the Greek ambience. He extended his empire in Ionia by demonstrations of amity and benevolence.

Alyattes was followed by his son Croesus (c.560-546). His legendary wealth enabled him to follow his father's example to give generous gifts to the oracle of Delphi. He helped to reconstruct the Artemisium at Ephesus which became his dependency and gradually all the other coastal cities fell to him. He opened his court to philosophers (including Solon, the legislator of Athens), architects and artists, as well as to wealthy businessmen and bankers. Sardis then became the financial metropolis of the Near East. But when a time of stress came upon Lydia in the person of Cyrus the Great of Persia, Croesus was abandoned by the Greeks, and independent Lydia fell and died (546). It was replaced by a Persian satrapy.

Lydia is just another example of the rise, glory and inevitable fall of all manifestations of life. Lydian civilization was but a continuation of its predecessors. The Phrygians, whose Great Mother goddess, Cybele, they had adopted (later inherited by Greece), taught them how to manufacture textiles with exotic designs, and skills in the production of beautiful jewellery, and other items of luxury. These luxuries gave them a reputation for a debilitating way of life. But Herodotus (I.94) points out that it was not very different from that of the Greeks. Lydia could be described as an important staging post for the transmission of the arts and sciences from the most ancient civilizations on their way to Greece.

Chronology: In Assyria, the years of the king's reign were currently noted by the yearly appointment of an official (*eponymous king),* who gave his name to the year. The office of this official was called *Limmu.* Of these officials of

the *Limmu*, we have long lists, dating from the reign of Adad-Nirari II (911-890) to that of Ashurbanipal (669-626), some of which give an account of events which happened during their year of office. [Henceforth paraphrased].
. . . Also, the *Limmu* official's name is given at the end of an account of events in a particular year, on cylinders and clay records of Assyrian history. The official's year of office, the 'Eponym', is extremely useful. For example, we are told that in the eponym of Pur-shagali [?], in the month of Sivan (May-June), there was an eclipse of the sun. This eclipse has been astronomically reckoned to have taken place in 763 and it correlates with the records of the *Limmu*.[25]

A fairly accurate picture of the times can be reconstructed from the surprisingly realistic sculptures which decorate the numerous monumental palaces and temples which the kings of Assyria erected to their own glory. A very important effect of Assyrian inheritance of the Babylonian Empire was the adoption of its wealthy culture. Among the enormous quantity of booty, large numbers of Babylonian cuneiform tablets were taken to Ashur. Interestingly, this obsession with the acquisition and imitation of a foreign culture, which continued down to the end of the Assyrian Empire (607), might reflect a sense of cultural inferiority, while at the same time showing a desire for learning which the Assyrians, perhaps too busy with their endless wars, seemed to be incapable of achieving.

However, this rather sweeping statement must be heavily qualified, for there are some very sensitive bronze reliefs, now at the British Museum, which adorned the walls of Ashurnasirpal II's and his son, Shalmaneser III's (c.880) palace at Nimrud or Calhu on the Tigris, as well as from the eighth century palace of Sargon II at Khorsabad, and a third group from the palace of Sennacherib and Ashurbanipal at Nineveh. The reliefs, about seven and sometimes nine feet high, would have decorated the interior of the buildings. Most of them depict military subjects, such as conquests and suppression of revolts; others are narratives in the form of a continuous frieze around the walls of the halls and chambers. In some instances there is an unexpected realism in the animated scenes, particularly of galloping horses drawing chariots in battle, and of horses in flight. There are some realistic, even poignant, depictions of hunted lions in their death throes. Mention must also be made of the gigantic winged, anthropomorphic animals of stone, guarding entrances of halls and palace chambers. Some monuments and some internal areas of buildings were painted on the mud-plaster surface of walls.

In these expressions of various forms of art, Ashurbanipal was among the foremost. He was also passionately interested in archaeology and collected an immense library at Nineveh of cuneiform tablets from all over his empire which, by chance, remained undamaged after the destruction of Assyria and Nineveh at the end of the seventh century. That library, a priceless legacy to posterity, is to the great credit of the otherwise cruel, pompous monarch. Because of it, he might now be rightly regarded as a man of some learning and sensitivity. The civilization revealed through these sources owes much to Babylon as well as to other conquered peoples, a fact which is explained by the exchange of goods and the traffic of different races which flowed within the vast, unified empire. But, reverting to the earlier statement of the apparent Assyrian *penchant* for war rather than the peacetime arts and sciences, one might wonder if many of the master artists and craftsmen were perhaps Babylonian immigrants or prisoners of War.

Ashurbanipal's death signalled the rapid collapse of his mighty empire. His successors are shadowy figures unable to maintain a tight control over their huge inheritance. Conspiracies and plots in the palace opened the gates to colonial defections. The Babylonians asserted their independence, and in 626 BC King Nabopolassar (625-605) founded a new Chaldean dynasty in Babylonia. Ten years later he went to war and all lower Mesopotamia rallied to his cause. The Assyrians were defeated at Arapkha (Kirkuk). The Egyptians, fearing in Babylonia a possible future enemy, sent reinforcements to the Assyrians, but in vain.

At the same time, the Medes, under their king, Cyaxares, attacked the region of the upper Tigris. In 614 they fell upon Ashur, the oldest capital of the empire, and sacked it. Nabopolassar joined Cyaxares in alliance with the Scythians, and, according to the Armenian historian, Moses of Khoren (who, in this instance, appears to have a good deal of credibility),[26] an Armenian contingent from Shupria, under their ruler, Paroyr, (assisting the Median commander-in-chief, Varbaces) attacked Nineveh, which succumbed after a heroic struggle. The last Assyrian king, Ashur-uballit II, still held out at Harran, as Pharaoh Necho II hastened from Egypt to support him.

For an inexplicable reason, in spite of guarantees of a peaceful march through Judaean territory, King Josiah would not allow Pharaoh Necho passage to the north. Josiah perished (609) on the bloody field of Megiddo (Armageddon) and Egypt was then able to proceed to Harran (II Kings XXIII. 29). But Necho's was a hollow victory, for he was a year too late to save his ally. In 607 the coalition had seized Harran. The Assyrian Empire had vanished without trace, from the pages of history for ever. The world had witnessed the end of another great empire. Nineveh was so thoroughly destroyed that a mere two hundred years later when Xenophon passed its site while leading his celebrated '10,000', he did not even notice a mound or an ancient remnant of Nineveh, which might have aroused his well-known keen curiosity.

THE CHALDEAN OR NEO-BABYLONIAN EMPIRE.[27] Nabopolassar had established the Neo-Babylonian empire. His son and successor, Nebuchadnezzar II (605-562), while still crown prince, pursued Pharaoh Necho towards Egypt. When he heard of his father's death, he abandoned his pursuit at Jerusalem, where he defeated Egypt's puppet king, razed the city, annexed Judaea and deported the Jews to Babylon into captivity (597 BC, 2 Kings XXV.21). He hastened back to Babylon to claim the throne. His empire included all the territories from the Egyptian border to the northern frontiers of Syria.

Judaea was merely required to pay tribute. Then, carried away by religious or nationalist fanaticism, in spite of the prophet Jeremiah's warnings, the tiny, insignificant Judea rebelled against its mighty master. It resulted in the first capture of Jerusalem (596) and the captivity of the Jewish king and a large number of his people. But the lesson was not learnt, and under King Zedekiah, in spite of Jeremiah's desperate cries, Judaea refused to pay tribute. In 507 Nebuchadnezzar's forces took Jerusalem for the second time; Zedekiah was taken captive, and in the presence of his lord, whom he had betrayed, he watched while his sons were slain, then his eyes were put out. The aristocracy was taken into captivity and, eventually, Jeremiah led the miserable remainder of the population to Egypt where Pharaoh Apries settled them in the foreign quarters of Daphnae.

Nebuchadnezzar was followed by his son who ruled for only two years. Then came the brief reign of a commoner who had married one of Nebuchadnezzar's daughters. Finally King Nabonidus (556-539), an Aramaean, seized the throne and inherited a corrupt and disintegrating Neo-Babylonian Empire.

King Nabonidus of Babylon (556-539), was not of the royal Chaldean line which had ended with the death of Nebuchadnezzar II. He was a usurper with a scholarly turn of mind, who was perhaps the respected intermediary to transact the peace treaty between Lydia and the Medes, almost 30 years before his accession. But his economic and social reforms in Babylon and his attempts to bring order out of the chaos into the kingdom he had inherited from his predecessors, brought about serious inflation – 50% rising to 200% – causing much distress to the people.[2] There were riots and disorder. His unpopularity was compounded by a plague which swept across the country, probably attributed by the hostile priesthood to the displeasure of the supreme god, Marduk, who had been degraded by Nabonidus when he had installed the moon-god, Sin, of Harran as the chief god.

Then, perhaps because of the tedium brought about by his ungrateful subjects, the king led an army out of Babylon, leaving his son Belshazar as his regent. He appears to have spent the next ten years in and around the oasis of Taima, in northwest Arabia, strategically situated to control the important trade routes crisscrossing the region between Egypt, Syria and the Persian Gulf. The real reasons for his departure from Babylon, and for his return to his old capital after ten years of absence, are unknown. He was back in time to preside over the New Year (539) celebrations in honour of the gods, which could not have been observed in the king's absence. According to the accounts given by Herodotus and Xenophon and the Book of Daniel, the festivities were prolonged, licentious and sacrilegious and the king himself (aged over 70 years) had been particularly offensive to the gods.

It was during these riotous celebrations that, having subdued the Lydians, Cyrus moved against the hitherto impregnable city of Babylon, with its double city-walls, complicated fortifications and the river Euphrates flowing through its centre. Herodotus (I.191) and Xenophon (VII.5) describe how Cyrus ordered the diversion of the river into a deep channel, cut by his sappers, before it entered the city. Babylon was a very large city; and it was now possible for the Persians to enter it by night along the dry riverbed; they surprised its defenders and seized it. Tradition based upon the Biblical version (Daniel V), has it that while this disaster hung over the Babylonian King Belshazzar (regent in his father's absence), he was indulging in excesses of debauchery, in his luxurious apartments amidst his concubines and courtiers. Surprised by the sudden appearance of the Persians he, his household and his palace guards were slaughtered mercilessly.

Historically, the Babylonians, tired of the careless government of their city, welcomed Cyrus as a deliverer. The old king, Nabonidus, fled. He was forced back by some Bedouins, to Babylon where he was perhaps killed. Others write that he was taken prisoner by Cyrus and treated well until his death. The history of Nabonidus, as told here, is a synopsis elicited from the ancient historians as well as recent writers. The curious reader is advised to consult the interesting and fuller accounts given by some of the authors listed at the end of this chapter, and others.

By showing his respect for Babylonian customs, gods and beliefs, Cyrus, a wise man, received the submission of the entire Chaldean or Neo-Babylonian Empire without striking a blow. He then restored to Babylon from Elam the effigies of their gods. He allowed the Judaeans to return to Jerusalem where he had generously rebuilt their temple and reinstated its holy relics. Although the Jews in Babylon were pleased to have such face-saving favours, many of them were far too prosperous to depart to the wilds of Judaea. But the ordinary Jewish folk in Judea who had not been deported, or those who had not followed Jeremiah into exile to Egypt, were, of course, grateful to their new master. The conquest of Babylon by Cyrus and the death of the last king of Babylon, Nabonidus (539), mark the end of the long history of Babylon, and herald a new phase in the Ancient History of the Near East.

Notes

1. Edwards I. E. S., The Early Dynastic Period in Egypt, CAH I². p. 43.
2. *Ibid.*
3. Oates Joan, *Babylon*, Thames & Hudson, London, 1979, p. 95.
4. Luckenbill D.D., *Ancient Records of Assyria and Babylon*, Chicago, 1926-27, quoted by Geordes Roux, *Iraq*, Penguin, London, 1980, p. 244.
5. Labat René, 'Elam and Western Persia, c.1200-1000 BC', *CAH II²*, p. 47.
6. Oates Joan, *Babylon, op. cit.* p. 101.
7. Astour M.C., *Orientalia XVIII*, 1969, pp. 318-414, quoted by G. Roux, *Iraq*, p. 257.
8. Diakonoff I. M., *The Prehistory of the Armenian People*, Caravan Books, New York, 1984.
9. Woolley Leonard, *Mesopotamia and the Middle East*, Methuen, London, 1961.
10. Hall H. R., *The Ancient History of the Near East*, London, 1963, p. 403.
11. Smith Sidney, 'The Foundations of the Assyrian Empire', CAH II¹, p. 10.
12. Munn-Rankin J.M., 'Assyrian Military Power, 1300-1200 BC', *CAH II²*, p. 282.
13. Smith Sidney, 'Senacherib and Eshaddon', *CAH II¹*, 1960, p. 74.
14. Oates Joan, op.cit., p. 109.
15. Oates Joan, op. cit., p. 111.
16. Frye R.N., *The Heritage of Persia*, Weidenfeld & Nicolson, 1965, pp. 65-7.
17. Sayce A.H., The Cuneiform Inscriptions of Van, *JRAS*, 1882, p. 412, and Frye, *ibid.*
18. Albright W.F., and Lambdin T.F., The Evidence of Language, CAH I⁴, p. 153.
19. Diakonoff I.M., *The Prehistory of the Armenian People, op. cit.*
20. Renfrew Colin, *Archaeology and Language*, Jonathan Cape, London, 1987.
21. Chahin M., *Some Legendary Kings of Armenia*, Third edition, Taunton, U.K. 1993.
22. Hogarth, *Lydia and Ionia*, CAH II¹. pp. 507-509.
23. Hogarth D.G., *ibid.* and Minns E.H., The Scythians and Northern Nomads, CAH II¹, p. 198.
24. Hall H. R., *The Ancient History of the Near East, op. cit.* p. 509, n. 1.
25. Hall H. R., *The Ancient History of the Near East, op. cit.*
26. Chahin M., *Some Legendary Kings of Armenia*, Third edition, U.K., 1993.
27. Saggs H.W.F., The Greatness that was Babylon, Sidgwick & Jackson, London, 1969, pp. 140-3

Chapter 10
The Persian Empire

The unfolding of history, as seen in the dramatic rise and decline, in turn, of earlier kingdoms, continues with the brief but catalytic appearance of the Indo-Aryan Medes. They were the largest of several small Indo-Aryan states, including the most important among them – the Persians. They had all migrated from the north into Iran during the second millennium BC. The Medes were the ancestors of Xenophon's Carduchi and the modern Kurds. From the 8th to the 6th centuries BC, they appear in the Bible and in Assyrian records, and later on in the Histories of Herodotus. The Median king, Deioces, seized and unified the small neighbouring (Persian) chieftainships whose people were racially and culturally related to the Medes (seventh century BC), thus creating a potent Median kingdom.

With Elam (the traditional, puissant buffer state between Assyria and possible invaders from the east) destroyed by Ashurbanipal, Cyaxares, son of Deioces, was able to lead a powerful, Median force into Assyria and, with Babylonian aid, he expunged it from the pages of history (607). He also overran Urartu (590), but was checked, at last, on the eastern bank of the river Halys by King Alyattes of Lydia. A war of attrition between the two powers having lasted five years (590-585), they decided to interpret the eclipse of the sun as a sign of the displeasure of the gods and forthwith called an armistice (585). The eclipse of the sun in that particular year had been predicted by Thales of Miletus (624-565). In his many travels, he is said to have

> learned of the 'Saronic cycle', that is to say the interval of 18 years and eleven days, a multiple of which the observations of ages of temple stargazers had shown to be usual between eclipses of the sun.[1]

The Halys river, then, was fixed as the boundary between the two combatants and peace was sealed by the marriage of the Lydian princess Aryênis, daughter of Alyattes, to Prince Astyages, son of King Cyaxares.

With Lydia now a client ally, the Median Empire stretched from beyond the Zagros Mountains in the east, over Mesopotamia and Asia Minor to the Mediterranean and the Aegean, far in the west. In 549, the Persians, under their own Cyrus II, King of Anshan (northern Elam) successfully revolted against his grandfather, Astyages, son of Cyaxares and seized his capital, Ecbatana (Hamadan), thus inheriting the immense Median Empire. Cyrus was the great-grandson of Teispes of the royal house of Achaemenes . Teispes had another great-grandson called Hystaspes, in line with his second son. The son of Hystaspes was called Darius.

Cyrus II, the Great, consolidated the vast Median empire, during the period of transition. He, a Persian, had already made an enemy of king Croesus of Lydia (560-546), son of Alyattes, who ruled the huge territory from the Aegean to the Halys river. For was not Astyages, son of Cyaxares, the Mede, the brother-in-law of Croesus, the enemy?

Cyrus and Croesus first joined in an indecisive battle near Sinope. Croesus retreated into his capital, Sardes, and disbanded his army against the approaching winter; for, in accordance with civilized tradition, men did not take part in war (the royal sport) out of season. But the Persians did not act according to such rules, and Cyrus suddenly appeared before the walls of Sardes. Croesus led out his remaining forces and was duly defeated and taken prisoner. But ultimately it all ended as a friendly match; Croesus not only survived Cyrus but later accompanied Cyrus' son, Cambyses, in his expedition against Egypt. After 540, the whole of Asia Minor recognised the sovereignty of Cyrus. (See Herod. I.77-88.)

Cyrus returned to his capital, Ecbatana. He was killed in battle against the Scyths in 530 in the Caucasdus region. He had restored and unified both Cyaxares's (Median) and Nebuchadnezzar's (Chaldean) empires under his own Persian rule and built, it seems, friendly relationships everywhere. His campaigns in the east, safeguarded the trade routes between the markets of Central Asia, India and Afghanistan, and the west. An important factor in the development of transport was the more extensive use of the Bactrian, two-humped camel, a pack animal used to cold climates and rough, even mountainous country; as opposed to the one humped dromedary of the Arabian deserts, which could be ridden for travel or warfare and also used for portage. The latter had been used by desert peoples for 3,000 years. The Assyrians might have brought the Bactrian variety to Mesopotamia early in the first millennium BC. The one-humped dromedary, which was well-known to the Egyptians, the Jews and Babylonians, was considered to be 'unclean' by the Assyrians and neglected. Again, it was the Assyrians who initiated its use, in their baggage trains early in the first millennium. However, the Persians must be credited with the adoption and regular use of both species, the Bactrian as beasts of burden and the dromedary mainly for riding. They were thus able to cross the Syrian desert, en route to the Mediterranean – an important short cut from Mesopotamia to the west.

The successor of Cyrus was his eldest son, Cambyses II (530-522). Cyrus had bequeathed the satrapies (governorships) of Armenia and Media to his second son, Bardiya (Xenophon, *Cyrop*. VIII.7.11). Bardiya has many names in Classical Greek tradition, and Bardes or Vardes coincides with the Armenian 'legendary' king P'aros or Pharos-Varos-Bar(d)os.[3] This interpretation of Bardiya's position after his father's death, as the governor of Armenia-Media, is important not only from the Armenian historical point of view, which legitimises the 'legendary' King P'aros, but especially because it gives the lie to the story of Dariu, a contender for the Persian throne, as told on his famous inscriptions on a cliff-face at Behistun, Kermanshah. That story alleges that Cambyses had secretly murdered his brother, Bardiya (next in line to the Persian throne), before departing on his Egyptian campaign, to ensure that his throne was not usurped in his absence; that after his departure (the inscriptions allege) a member of the Magi, called Gaumata, had lied and said that he was Bardiya. As few people had ever seen Bardiya – he was stationed in faraway Armenia– and because those who had were fearful for their own lives at the hands of Darius, 'Gaumata' was accepted as the legitimate king.

Then, seven conspirators, led by Darius, son of Hystaspes and his accomplice, Hydarnes (the inscriptions continue), entered the palace and 'slew Gaumata' (the false Bardiya). And Darius proclaimed himself King of Persia. That is the gist of the inscriptions. The truth is that Cambyses did not murder his brother, and that Bardiya, satrap of Armenia, the legitimate heir, succeeded Cambyses, after the latter's death on his way back from Egypt. Bardiya was in fact king for just under a year in 522, before he was actually murdered by Darius and his accomplices. Darius I (522-486) then seized the throne of the Persian Empire, and high on the smooth face of a cliff at Behistun, he had his own version of the story inscribed in three languages, Elamite, Akkadian (Babylonian) and Old Persian, in three different cuneiform scripts, alleging that he and his fellow conspirators had deposed Gaumata, a pretender to the throne. And so the royal line of Achaemenes-Teispes-Hystaspes flourished.

Something must be said about this fabulous memorial to Darius I, the Great, King of Kings, ruler of the vast Persian Empire, inscribed on a towering cliff, 6,000 ft. high at Behistun or Bisitun. It could not be reached because the ledge on which the scribes had stood had been cut away after they had completed their work. So the inscriptions have survived for 2,500 years. But in the 1840's Henry Creswicke Rawlinson, a determined scholar and army officer, later British consul at Baghdad, and one of the trustees of the British Museum, prepared to risk his life, stood on a remaining narrow ledge, no more than 18 wide, just below the inscriptions, and made a precise copy of part of them. Between 1847 and 1857, he even deciphered the Old Persian and Babylonian texts. In 1904 a cradle was hung from a ledge above the inscriptions from which a complete, revised copy of the trilingual text was made by Leonard W. King and R. Campbell Thompson.[3]

Not for the first or the last time in history, success and power wipe out dishonour, especially if they can be hidden behind a lie. Once the usurper, Darius the Great, son of Hystaspes, had gained control of the empire (522), he described, in the Behistun inscriptions, how he reorganised it into satrapies or governorships (Herod III.89-96 mentions 20, but there were at least three more). Each satrap was practically a viceroy who wielded every power within his province, except (officially) command over the army, which was reserved to officers who took their orders directly from the Great King. There were also inspectors – 'the eyes and ears of the king'.

If the satrap was a native prince, he could mobilise his own people against the Persian army, when a rebellion was intended. And a great rebellion there certainly was, soon after Darius ascended the throne. The whole empire flared up; the powerful satraps in Mesopotamia and Anatolia rose up in arms. However, by 517 he had subdued them all, and was fully in control of the empire, with all the satrapies intact. These momentous events, too, are described in the inscriptions.

Easy, efficient communications were essential, for the proper administration of a world empire stretching from India to the Aegean, the Levant and Egypt. These were made accessible by a series of roads for the king's messengers, the most famous of which was the great Royal Road from the capital, Susa, to Sardis and the Aegaean ports of Smyrna and Ephesus, a distance of some 2,000 miles. It is recorded that the king's messengers covered the distance from Susa to Sardis (1,680 miles) in 18 days, against an ordinary merchant's 90 days. There were 111 post houses at intervals of ten to fifteen miles.

But an emperor's ambitions are insatiable. There was still the Scythian threat from the north. It was during his Scythian wars that Cyrus the Great had been killed. From around the Aral Sea and the steppes of southern Russia as far west as the Danube Delta, they prospered on trade with the Greek colonies on the north coast of the Black Sea, especially those on the great rivers - the Dniester, the Don and the Bug. Darius could not reach them over the barrier of the Caucasus. With his huge army of 700,000 men he, therefore, crossed the Bosphorus, then the Danube over a bridge of boats, in pursuit of them. Their horsemen harassed the Persians from all sides.

For fear of his army running short of food and supplies, Darius was obliged to turn back. But his foray had not been entirely in vain for he had made himself master of the Straits, and of Thrace, as far as the borders of Macedon. Macedonia had no choice but to recognise the Great King's overlordship. He also reasserted Persian sovereignty over the Greek Ionian city states along the Aegean coast. This enabled his powerful fleet to cut off supplies of wheat to the Greek mainland, from Asia and southern Russia, Egypt and Libya, as well as gold from the Urals and Siberia and, very importantly, timber, required for the construction of Athenian ships.

During the 500 years down to the times of Darius, the people on the mainland of Greece, especially the city of Athens, powerfully influenced by the Ionian city states, strung along the western coast of Asia Minor, had built a considerable civilization, with maritime trading interests. There were power-struggles between the Greek city-states, but particularly so between Athens and Sparta, a military aristocracy in the Peloponnesus.

In spite of the frightful Persian danger overshadowing Greece, Athens and Sparta continued their endless wars and rivalries with one another. The Spartans were anti-Persian; the Athenians generally were prepared to accept the Persian overlordship. The Athenians awoke to the awful implications of such a policy and the proximity of their danger when the Persians introduced their gold to bribe the mainland Greeks for their own ends. Athens then made common cause with Sparta and her other Greek rivals against Persia.

That policy encouraged the Ionians to rebel, relying on help from mainland Greece; the Ionic League was re-established (499); Athens sent troops and the allies besieged Sardis; Persian reinforcements drove off the insurgents and, ultimately, the revolt was crushed. Among other cities that were captured by the Persians, Miletus fell (492) after a siege of two years, many of its citizens were deported to a place near the mouth of the river Tigris and a Persian satrap was placed over the remaining population. Chios and Lesbos were taken, the young men were castrated and the girls sent to the Persian harems; Byzantium and

Chalcedon were given to the flames.

Darius then decided to invade mainland Greece, friend of the Ionians. Before doing so, he tried to persuade the Democratic party in Athens to side with him in return for his support of them to regain office. This offer having been refused, the city-state of Eretria, ally of Athens, was besieged and captured. But the commander in charge of the Persians, a Median, instead of negotiating an understanding with the Democrats, burnt the temples, destroyed the town and sent all the inhabitants to Susa into slavery. They were settled,

> in a place called Ardericca, 210 furlongs from Susa, where salt, bitumen and oil were extracted and here they continued to my time (c 440), and still they spoke their own language, and remembered their [Greek)]origin. (Herod. VI.119)

The Greek Conservative and Democrat factions, realising at last the foolishness of division, joined forces. When the Persians landed at Marathon they were confronted by an Athenian army, under Miltiades. The decisive battle of Marathon (490) was then fought and won by Greece. Seven enemy ships were captured and the Persian army withdrew, leaving 6,000 dead while the Athenians suffered a loss of only 192 killed. It was a glorious victory. The battle of Marathon had saved the Athenians' very homes from the domination of a foreign power. A huge moral stimulant, it also proved that the dreaded Persian force was not invincible. On the Persian side, it was merely a small loss of prestige, barely a pinprick in the colossal Empire's vanity. But in the last analysis Darius' ambition had been thwarted by the foolish action of his Median general, who had treated the city and citizens of Eretria so savagely. But for that barbarity, which had united the warring Greeks, the Persian campaign might have been successful. Among the great names that appear in Athens at this time, that of Themistocles must be remembered in the world of politics and war strategy. Anticipating a second Persian invasion to avenge the failure of the first, he cajoled and finally persuaded his compatriots to build a large and powerful fleet.

On his way to crush a rebellion in Egypt, Darius died (486). His son Xerxes (486-464) inherited a vast empire to administer, colonial rebellions in Egypt and many other parts of the Empire to suppress, and the humiliation of a defeat in European Greece to avenge. As viceroy of Babylon, Xerxes suppressed a revolt of the Babylonian satrap with ferocity, destroying the city walls and fortifications, pillaging and razing the temples, melting down the golden effigy of the god Bel and demoting the political status of Babylon among the satrapies by withdrawing his own title of 'king of Babylon' and substituting the historically more precise 'king of the Medes and Persians'. He then crushed the Egyptian rebellion with the utmost brutality and left Egypt with a simmering hatred of Persian rule, which would one day explode.

Having achieved peace in his realms, Xerxes had no wish to begin new imperial adventures. Like some other rulers whose ferocity towards their subjects verged upon sadism, as in the case of Assyria's Ashurbanipal, he had artistic inclinations and an appreciation of beauty, a luxurious court life and the company of beautiful women. He planned to build monuments and palaces and, like his father, to inscribe his achievements in stone, not only in his own cities of Susa and Persepolis, but in other parts of his empire too. For example, in his Armenian Satrapy, high on the south cliff of the citadel at Van, and 'inaccessible, but easily legible on account of the size and distinctness of its letters, by a glass from below'[4] (a telescope) Layard copied Xerxes' inscription, which reads:

> A great god is Ormuzd, who is the greatest of gods, who has created this earth, who has created that heaven, who has created mankind, who has given happiness to man, who has made Xerxes king, sole king of many kings, sole lord of many. I am Xerxes, the great king, the king of kings, the king of the provinces with many tongues, the king of this great earth far and near, son of king Darius the Achaemenian. Says Xerxes the king: Darius the king, my father, did many works through the protection of Ormuzd, and on this hill he commanded to make his tablet and an image; yet an inscription he did not make. Afterwards I ordered this inscription to be written. May Ormuzd, and all the other gods, protect me and my kingdom and my works.

However, against his inclinations, Xerxes was persuaded by the 'hard right' as we would describe aggressive political parties today, to avenge his father's defeat in Greece. The huge war machine was set in motion. A bridge of boats was built to span the Hellespont, which the great host took no less than seven days to cross. Thrace, Macedon and Thessaly and most of northern Greece submitted.

Athens, Sparta and all rival parties sank their perpetual quarrels in the face of the approaching enemy. It was the Spartans this time who took the initiative. Leonidas, with 300 warriors undertook to hold the Persian host at the pass of Thermopylae, thus providing enough time for Athens to prepare for the worst. A memorable and heroic stand was made by the Spartans at the Pass. But a treacherous peasant guided the Persians behind the Greek lines, and Leonidas and his loyal band were slaughtered to a man..

Abandoned by the inhabitants, Attica and Athens were overrun by the Persians and set ablaze. The Acropolis was reduced to ashes. The Athenians, who had at last taken the advice of Themistocles, had their ships ready, and the Greek fleet took its position to defend the Isthmus at Salamis. Xerxes had himself installed upon a throne on a cliff to watch the great sea battle; it was the year 480 BC, ten years after his father's defeat. At the end of the contest, the Persian fleet was destroyed; the king, humiliated and under the influence of uncontrollable anger, had the Phoenician admiral of his fleet put to death. This provoked the powerful Phoenician contingent as well as the Egyptian ships to abandon the Persians. The desperate Xerxes departed to Asia.

The Persian land forces then gathered at Plataea to meet the reformed Greek army. The Persian commander-in-chief rashly decided to lead his men himself, and he was killed. The Persians, then retreated depending on the remaining ships of their fleet for supplies from Asia. Unfortunately for them, on the very day when they had been defeated at Plataea, a force of Athenians had attacked the Persian fleet sheltering at Mycale and destroyed it (479). Then the combined armies of mainland Greeks and the Ionians drove out the Persians from Europe, beyond the Straits, for ever.

More space has been given to this particular struggle between Greece and Persia than to any other. Some scholars suggest that the course of European history was changed, and others even go so far as to assert that Europe itself might have been orientalised if the Persians had been victorious! If the fortunes of war, which are so often decided (as in this struggle) by the incompetence and inter-rivalries of commanders, had favoured the Persians, it is most likely that for a brief period Greece would have been put under a satrap and made to pay tribute. But it could not have been held for long; the distance from Persia was much too great, there were large numbers of Greek sympathisers all over western Asia, there were always intrigues and disunity in the Persian court (as in all high places, at all times) and communications were slow. In such circumstances, sooner or later, the Persians would have been either driven out, or obliged to abandon Europe of their own accord.

It is far beyond the scope of this work to say any more about Greece. Whole libraries of books have been written on the many aspects of its civilisation, initially inherited from Asia, which ultimately travelled to Western Europe, via the Roman Empire. But because the expression 'democracy' is bandied about so much in our own times and always associated with Greece, perhaps a comment or two on it ought to be offered

Sir Moses Finley writes (*Annales*) that

British scholars had for long sentimentalised Athens. They attributed modern notions of liberty and democracy to a society that was imperialist and rested on slavery. We should accept that far from handing down to us eternal truths, Greece and Rome were 'other'– as unlike our own culture as that of an African tribe or Polynesian islanders.[5]

The Concise Oxford Dictionary defines 'democracy' as:

(State practising) government by the people, direct or representative.

H G Wells:

The Demos was government by the whole body of the citizens, by the many as distinguished from the few. But let the modern reader mark that word 'citizen:. The slave was excluded, the freedman was excluded, the stranger; even the Greek born in the city, whose father had come eight or ten miles from the city beyond the headland, was excluded. The earliest democracies (but not all) demanded a property qualification from the citizen, and property in those days was land . . . but the modern reader will grasp that here was something very different from modern democracy. At the end of the fifth century BC this property qualification had been abolished in Athens, for example; but Pericles a great Athenian statesman . . . had established a law (451 BC) restricting citizenship to those who could establish Athenian descent on both sides. Thus, in the Greek democracies quite as much as in the oligarchies, the citizens form a close corporation, ruling sometimes, as in the case of Athens in its great days, a big population of slaves and 'outlanders'.[6]

Wells goes on to comment that 'if suddenly a modern man was spirited back to the extremist Greek democracy, he would regard it as a kind of oligarchy' (government by a few). In fact most Greek city-states, starting with those in Ionia, were governed by oligarchies which were probably at first aristocracies. But 'democracy', as the expression is understood by most people today, means rule by the representatives of everyone living within the territory of a nation, through a voting system which installs them in an institution called Parliament. This form of leadership, if incorrupt, would seem to be the most satisfactory form of government, reflecting the image of a highly civilized, responsible and informed people. It is impossible to apply such a form of government fairly to countries with untutored, ignorant populations, burdened with centuries of tribal shibboleths as often happens so disastrously in our times. For such new states, it seems that the best form of government is a benevolent dictatorship or, at best, a benevolent oligarchy. But it has to be benevolent. One wonders, however, if 'oligarchy' and 'benevolent' are not, with few exceptions, mutually exclusive terms, for, unfortunately, oligarchies are often amoral plutocracies.

In the Middle Ages and down to the nineteenth century AD, contests for power were expressed in chronic dynastic warfare, as well as by arranged marriages of royal and aristocratic families. Nationalism, a tragic modern phenomenon, sets millions of peoples, armed with the most horrific weapons ever devised, against each other for acquiring territories rich in raw materials and cheap labour, for the benefit of the rulers; seldom for the alleviation of poverty of millions, who themselves, or their sons and fathers, fight and die in support of their rulers' often misguided, overambitious or corrupt policies.

In ancient times, which is our main concern, government was by hereditary royal dictatorship, and war was waged to acquire more territory, more wealth, more power for the king, the aristocracy and the temple priests. The struggles were between kings; the people of the victor sometimes benefited from 'the crumbs' of the wealth seized by their ruler. I have digressed from the main line of my narrative in an attempt to correct the idea that democracy, in its ideal sense, was a universal form of government in ancient Greece. It was achieved for a brief period in Athens, but in some other Greek cities, it flickered for a moment and died. Greek city-states were at first sometimes governed by 'tyrants' or dictators and later mainly by oligarchies.

> It was not, however, either in Sparta or in Athens, but rather in the brilliant necklace of Ionian cities, which had been strung along the coast of Asia Minor as a consequence of the great migration, that the true centre of Greek civilization was to be found in the seventh and sixth centuries before Christ. In art and philosophy, in trade and civilization, Miletus was a pioneer in that astounding development of the human faculties, speculative, artistic, and practical, which we recognize as distinctively Hellenic. At a time when the rough tribal invaders of the north were destroying the old Mycenaean civilization on the mainland of Greece, *the Ionians of Asia Minor and the islands, preserved what was precious in the older culture, and assimilating also the customs of the nearer east* (my italics), deriving a coinage from the Lydians, and a system of astronomy from Babylon and Egypt, made rapid advances in the arts of Peace.[7]

The disastrous second Persian invasion, under Xerxes in 480, was a serious psychological setback for him. He retired to Persepolis where he resumed his building projects and completed the unfinished works of his father. He was assassinated in the luxurious surroundings of his palace in 461. Persepolis, after nearly 2,500 years, is still a wonderful monument to Persian civilization, in spite of the destruction of an extensive part of it by Alexander the Great 250 years later (331).

Henceforth, there is a slow decline in the power and culture of Iran. Although the intrigues and wars with Greece continued, there was never again the same dedication for the conquest of the European mainland. The wars with Egypt also continued with varying fortunes. It is, therefore, appropriate that something should be said about the art and culture of Persia, during the reign (particularly) of Darius, and that of his son, Xerxes.

The hoard of fine gold objects, known as the Ziwiye Treasure (c. 650), showed great advances in artistic techniques and evolution from the earlier periods – a leap from dreams to the reality of inspired waking hours. And when such a metaphor is used to describe the evolution of artistic excellence, then parallel social advances in physical comforts, variety of foods and entertainment, as well as the niceties of social behaviour, must be taken for granted.

Yet another hoard, the Oxus Treasure, now exhibited at the British Museum, 'is mainly Achaemenian in style, and is one of the most important groups of material of the period. The objects may have come from a cache of precious goods hidden at some troubled time, or else may represent the accumulated wealth of offerings made at a temple or shrine.'[8]

The collection was found in 1880, when

Captain F.C. Burton, a British political officer resident near Kabul, daringly rescued three merchants who had been captured by bandits. They had with them a rich collection of fine gold and silver which they said had been found three years before in the dry bed of the Oxus River, and which they were taking to sell in India . . . Although it is generally accepted that the Oxus Treasure came from a single hoard, the details are unknown, and there is some uncertainty as to its original significance . . . One theory is that the Treasure represents the accumulated wealth of a temple – perhaps that of the goddess Anahita, who is known to have had an important shrine in the area. Confirmation of this theory is seen in the numerous small strips of gold, roughly incised with figures of people and animals, which can only be simple votive gifts given as offerings to the deity.

Whatever its original significance, the Treasure is an important collection of objects illustrating various styles of art, techniques of manufacture, and other aspects of Iranian society between the 6th and 3rd centuries BC – and some are perhaps earlier. The finely embossed gold scabbard, for example, decorated with scenes copied from Assyrian relief sculpture (compare examples on display in the Assyrian Saloon) may be an example of the art of the Medes. Most of the items are Achaemenian Persian, but a few show the distinctive features of other art-styles.

Notable among these are the complex shapes and flowing curves associated with the art of the nomadic Scythians. A few items, such as finger-rings, show Greek influence, and were probably made by Greek craftsmen resident at the Persian court.

The Achaemenian Persians were famous in antiquity for their wealth and the magnificence of dress and adornment worn by the king and nobility. Gold armlets, collars, and other ornaments were used to indicate status, and often were presented as marks of favour. The Treasure of the Oxus provides ample confirmation of this wealth, as well as being a basic source for the study of ancient Persian art.[9]

Reference has already been made to Darius' and Xerxes' magnificent architectural achievements; the most celebrated examples of that cultural heritage are to be found in the palace complex of buildings and monuments at Persepolis. They show certain features which were probably adopted from 'the Assyrians, such as raised platforms, sculptured monsters, slabs of bas-relief, besides glazed and coloured brickwork which it is their glory to have brought to perfection'. The following by Mr Charles Burney, is a brief description of Persepolis:[10]

Achaemenid architecture appears in its purest form at Persepolis (Parsa), for at Susa something of Mesopotamian traditions survived in the plan of the palace: the glazed brick relief figures of the imperial guard, the Immortals, in the palace of Artaxerxes II (404-359 BC) are in the Assyro-Babylonian tradition; and rooms were grouped round internal courts. The terrace of Persepolis, covering thirteen hectares, is partly cut out of the mountain and partly artificial. The buildings date to the reigns of Darius the Great, Xerxes and Artaxerxes I (i.e. to c. 518-460 BC) and comprise public halls and residential palaces, rather loosely related to one another. The function, recently much discussed, of Persepolis centred probably round a rather brief annual residence by the king over the period of the great New Year spring festival. The reliefs emphasise the international character of an empire whose civilization has been all too much belittled by the bias of philhellenic western scholars unwilling to look for once westwards through eastern eyes, instead of always vice versa. The reliefs of the Audience Hall or Apadana (hall of many columns) demonstrate the cosmopolitan character of the empire which embraced Egypt and Bactria, Ionia and India. The design of the Apadana shows the innovation of columnar architecture, a major contribution of the Achaemenid kings. When Persepolis went up in flames at the feast of the Macedonian conqueror, a world lasting several millennia finally expired.[10]

This detailed description of the truly sumptuous buildings at Persepolis proves that there were forerunners of the beautiful temples, theatres and monuments of the Periclean Acropolis at Athens.

The palace of Darius 'is a remarkable structure 1,500 ft .by 1,000 ft in extent and 40ft above the plain, partly hewn out of solid rock and partly built up of large blocks of solid stone, laid without mortar but held together by metal cramps. The approach on the northwest was by a magnificent flight of steps, 22 ft. wide, shallow enough for horses to ascend. The Propylaea by Xerxes formed a monumental entrance, flanked by man-made bulls and massive piers glowing in glazed bricks, and through this gateway passed foreign ambassadors, subject princes, and royal retinues to the palaces on the platform. Among these stood the Hypostyle Hall of Xerxes, which was an impressive structure, and the 'Hall of the Hundred Columns' built by Darius, which, according to Plutarch, was burnt by Alexander the Great. It was probably the audience hall or throne room of the palace and was 225 ft square, enclosed by a brick wall, 11 ft thick, in which there were some 44 doorways and windows. The walls flanking the entrance portico were enlivened with topical bas-reliefs representing the king with his retinue receiving ambassadors. The flat cedar roof was supported upon 100 columns, 37 ft high, of which only one remains in situ, and they recall the hypostyle halls of Egyptian temples, but have a character all their own with moulded bases, fluted shafts, and curious, complex capitals with vertical Ionic-like volutes and twin bulls supporting the roof-beams.

'The palace of Darius, the earliest built on the platform, was rectangular in plan with a portico of sixteen columns. The stone lintels and jambs of doors and windows, as well as the bases of the portico columns, still exist, though the rubble walls have crumbled away. The palace of Xerxes, though it consisted only of a central hall and three columned porticoes, was of great size, with an area of some 24,000 square ft. The palace was further raised on a podium 10 ft high, reached by four flights of steps. Columns of porticoes and hall, which originally numbered

72, though only 17 remain, were 65 ft. high with bell-shaped bases and fluted shafts. Those of the north portico and great hall had elaborate capitals of Ionic volutes set on end and surmounted by double bulls, while those of the east and west porticoes consisted only of double bulls or griffins. Flower gardens, orange groves, and summer pavilions formed the luxurious surroundings of the luxurious palaces.[11]

ARTAXERXES I (464-425) son of Xerxes, came to the throne in a turmoil of assassinations and killings by his rebellious and conspiratorial brothers. Athens, short of wheat from the northern granaries, allied herself with insurgent Egypt against Persia. The rising was put down by the Great King: the Athenian fleet was destroyed by fire in the Nile Delta. An alliance between Sparta and Athens against Persia restored peace. The Ionian cities were freed and the Persian forces were pushed beyond the Halys river.

This, the middle of the fifth century, was the Golden Age of Athens when that city was fortunate in producing a leader, Pericles, who not only possessed ideals but also the gold with which to implement them. The Delian League (a military alliance of which Pericles was the president) had intended the gold of its members for defence purposes. The Acropolis was rebuilt in marble. Its temples and amphitheatres, its statues in the round as well as reliefs, all beautiful in their classical, dignified simplicity, are still admired and imitated all over the Western world. The gates of Athens were thrown open and men of genius and talent, even from distant countries, such as India, are said to have visited Athens. The Greeks themselves travelled all over the ancient world, and learnt at first hand more of the accumulated riches of oriental knowledge; the thoughts of philosophers, a number of whom had travelled to various countries stretching from Sicily and Egypt to Babylon and Persia, were discussed in the academies of Athens and its populated squares. The plays of great writers were performed in its theatres. In the field of science, Babylonian scholarship, for example, inspired Democritus of Miletus to develop his atomic theory. Documents of Egyptian and Mesopotamian origin show that the scientific disciplines of medicine and mathematics were at least a thousand years earlier than the first Greek records of those studies.[12]

Social and political reforms, lead to the triumph of Athenian democractic rule by the consensus of the whole (small, native, select) population of the city (made possible by the labour of slaves); this has never been attained since, although much lip-service is paid by some of today's quasi-plutocracies in favour of that form of government. In singing our admiration of the exceptional, collective genius which created classical Athens, it must be remembered that it was the epoch of 3,000 years of Near Eastern cultural development which reached mainland Greece chiefly via Anatolia and the Ionian city-states. These events took place at a time of social maturity, a century before the destruction of the First Persian Empire (331). Asia and Europe extended their cultural relationships. Herodotus (c.484-c.425) travelled widely, and wrote his great *History*, which is still a mainly reliable source-book not only for events of his own times, but also for many happenings before his days, as told to him by learned men that he met on his travels.

Figure 38. Cylinder-seal and impression: King Darius the Great in his chariot hunting lions. The inscription gives his name in three languages. c.500 BC. Courtesy, Trustees of the British Museum.

From Babylonia, Ezra had been allowed to lead 1,500 Jewish families to Palestine (Ezra II). Inevitably, feuds had followed between the 'foreign' newcomers and the Palestinian 'natives' whose ancient traditions had not previously been interrupted. Eventually, through the statesmanship and legislation of Ezra and the intervention of the Great King's ambassador, Nehemiah, the Jews settled down as loyal subjects of Persia. Jerusalem's walls were rebuilt (441) and the high priest also assumed temporal powers as ruler of Juda`ea – Nehem II.

Under Artaxerxes I, there were serious rifts in the Empire's web.The growth of political and military power and confidence of mainland Greece and Ionia, and revolts and dismemberment of important colonies, such as Syria and Babylonia, emphasise Persia's troubled political predicament.

DARIUS II Nothus (424-404): When Darius II ascended the throne, the Peloponnesian Wars (between Athens and Sparta 431-404), which did so much damage to cultural growth, had been in progress for seven years. Persian bribes and conspiracy had incited the two ancient rivals to take up arms once more against one another, weakening them both *vis-à-vis* their traditional enemy, the Persian Empire, which was still the most powerful military force, in terms of its seemingly inexhaustible resources. But it has to be remembered that nationalism is a modern political concept, and that in the past, city-states were, most of the time, independent of one another and jealous of each other's wealth and achievements; ready to partake in conspiracies within their own circles, even siding with cities or countries whose cultural and linguistic backgrounds were completely alien to them. In the midst of a succession of uprisings in Sardis and the Ionian states, which were supported by Athens, Darius, allied with Sparta, regained control of those Asiatic Greek city-states and a treaty confirmed Persian suzerainty over them.

There also occurred a successful rising in Egypt against its Persian masters. The Spartans, as allies of Persia, at first sustained a disastrous defeat. Their fleet was destroyed by Egypt's ally, Athens. The Persians replaced it with new warships, which the Spartans used to blockade the Straits. Thus, deprived of wheat, Athens was forced to capitulate.

ARTAXERXES II (404-358): Darius II died in 404. At the coronation of Artaxerxes II at Passargadae his brother, Cyrus (known as Cyrus the Younger), thrust a dagger into him. Cyrus, already favoured by the satrapies and armies of large portions of western and central Asia Minor, still aimed at the throne. The attempted assassination failed. It says much for the forbearance of Artaxerxes that he listened to the supplications of his mother and not only allowed his brother to go free but also to continue with his prestigious power in Asia Minor. Such leniency is

Figure 39. Gold and lapis lazuli handle of a lonog staff. From West Iran, Median or Early Achaemenian. c.7th-6th centuries BC. Ht. 19.5 cm. Courtesy, Trustees of the British Museum.

interpreted by worldly historians as weakness of character.

Then, the ambitious and dishonourable Cyrus showed his 'strength of character' by taking up arms against his brother. Xenophon was among his troops, when, in battle, Cyrus once more nearly succeeded in murdering his brother. It would have been imprudent of the Great King to ignore that second attempt upon his life. During the night following that first day of war, when the rebel troops and officers were asleep, Artaxerxes' men slaughtered Cyrus and all his officers. Xenophon contrived to lead away the remaining 10,000 troops on his celebrated march across Armenia to the Black Sea. It is said that if Cyrus had succeeded in seizing the throne, his initiative and energy would have saved the imminent downfall of the Persian Empire.

There were rebellions all over the Empire which were somehow contained not always by Persian military forces as by Persian gold, which was readily available in large quantities, as we have seen, to bribe this or that army, city or country to side with the Great King against the current enemy. Egypt, however, rebelled and remained independent. Encouraged by this, as well as the exploits of Xenophon, Sparta invaded Asia Minor. But successes and conquests were halted and Sparta withdrew when Athens took up arms in support of the Persians.

Both the rival cities were now too exhausted to defy Persia when the Great King imposed 'the shameful King's Peace', the Peace of Antalcidas (387) between Persia and Greece which gave Persia all the Greek cities in Asia Minor, as well as Cyprus; all other Greek cities were to be independent. The ambassadors of Athens and Sparta had no choice but to submit. The taxes imposed upon the Ionian cities by Persia, however, were much lighter than those they had to pay in turn to their 'liberators', Athens and Sparta. Incorporated within the thriving and uninterrupted economy of the vast Empire, they became as prosperous as ever. But Artaxerxes had to settle scores with his erstwhile enemies on the Greek mainland.

Incited by Persian gold, Thebes (Greece) attacked and smashed Athens and Sparta, its former, and now exhausted, enemies. Thus was Hellas torn and conquered by diplomacy and gold, where the immense armies and navvies of Darius and Xerxes had failed.

Now here was Artaxerxes, Great King, at last dominant and apparently invincible, yet, he was not to end his days in peace. The governors or satraps of the 20 or more provinces, inherited from his forebears, had become very powerful and restive. A few of the mightiest had always been hereditary satraps, particularly if their founders had been members of the royal family (as Orontes of Armenia, who had married the king's daughter), or on the topmost rung of the aristocracy (as Hydarnes, commander of the 'Immortals', who had been the accomplice of Darius I). Such satraps with royal connections had probably increased with the passage of time, as a result of the king's policy to reinforce his power. In the time of Artaxerxes, the king's inspectors, the 'eyes and ears' of the king, were, however, probably only a memory or completely ineffectual.

The Empire was no longer stable. It had sustained irreversible defeat in Egypt and that country had proclaimed its independence. As the years of struggle succeeded each other, Phoenicia and Syria, too, gained their freedom. There was discontent among the peasantry and the unprivileged throughout the Empire. They were prepared to follow new masters who promised them better living conditions. The satraps and their armies laid waste the countryside in their wars against one another; in the increasing turmoil, one by one, all the countries west of the Euphrates rose up in rebellion. Some of these satraps rallied under the most powerful of them. Among the latter, Orontes of Armenia assumed the leadership of the rebels. He even struck his own gold coins and seemed to be aiming for the throne. The vast Empire appeared to be on the point of disintegration.

The situation was saved because of the disunity of the satraps themselves, who took sides and fought one another for more power, more territory and more influence. Egypt allied with Sparta, for example, threatened Syria; Datames of Cappadocia seized the Greek cities on the Black Sea coast. He, too, minted his own coinage. He was assassinated at a counsel of rebesatraps. Again the situation quickly changed in favour of the Great King when Egypt's Pharaoh deserted his allies, in order to crush a rebellion of his own subjects. When Orontes, in turn, betrayed his accomplices, peace of a kind was re-established. The king forgave Orontes who retired to his estates in Mysia where he ended his days in luxury and peace (which are not always complimentary). The countryside was ravaged by armed bands of robbers and it seethed with local uprisings against satrap or aristocrat. In the midst of that universal carnage and disorder, Artaxerxes II at last died, after a reign of almost fifty years (404-358).

ARTAXERXES III (358-338) was certainly cast in a different mould from that of his father. Although as bloodthirsty and as cruel, he possessed a stronger character and a determination which was unshakable. He first executed several brothers and sisters (possible claimants to the throne), and he disciplined the satraps; he reconquered rebellious Egypt, whose Pharaoh fled to Ethiopia. The Empire was restored, apparently to its early glories.

The wars and the threat of war with Greece came to an end when king Philip of Macedonia and his son Alexander conquered the whole of Greece in 338. But in that same year Artaxerxes was assassinated and the murderers could not have realised that they had struck down the one person capable of successfully confronting Alexander the Great, who was soon to appear in Asia. But before that momentous event, the son of Artaxerxes, Arses, had reigned for two years and died of poison. A member of the other branch of the Achaemenid line had then ascended the throne.

DARIUS III (Codomannus) (336-330) was as capable an emperor as most of his predecessors; but his fatal mistake was to underestimate the military genius who was to destroy his empire. Alexander the Great was already master of a rebellious Greece which, contrary to Alexander's desire to be considered as a Greek, recognised him only as a foreign conqueror. His father, Philip, had himself been a great admirer of Athenian scholarship and was determined to associate his small kingdom of Macedon with Greece. He opened his court to learned men of his day and provided Alexander with Greek teachers, among them Euripides and Aristotle. The young Alexander also read the plays of Sophocles, Aeschylus and others. In short, he was steeped in Greek culture.

After his father's death he decided to carry out Philip's ambition to avenge the Persian invasion of Greece. Without the support of the Greek fleet or the goodwill of the Greeks themselves, Alexander crossed the Dardanelles (Hellespont) and was met at the River Granicus by a contingent of Persians, sent by the disdainful Darius to wipe out the impertinent young invader. The Persian force was destroyed at that first confrontation (May, 334). This was to be the pattern of encounters on an increasingly large scale; the traditional Persian military loose formations could not withstand the tightly disciplined Macedonian phalanx, its highly trained men armed with the fearsome 'sarissa', a spear about 18 ft. long.

Alexander's general plan was to occupy the Ionian cities, and march round the coast of the Mediterranean, taking all the great ports and isolating the Persian fleet. He quickly achieved this in Asia Minor, in spite of the defence put up by Miletus and Halicarnassus, and the less troublesome Caria, Lycia and Pisidia who could not see Alexander as a liberator, but rather as another conqueror whose suzerainty would be more demanding in taxes than the ancient Persian masters, who seem to have been moderate in this respect.

In the summer of 333, having negotiated the Taurus mountains, Alexander emerged from the narrow pass which opened into Cilicia. A cavalry dash by the Persian satrap, Arsames, saved Tarsus from destruction. It was now urgently necessary to press southwards along the Syria-Palestinian coast to capture the important Phoenician coastal cities, essential bases of the Persian fleet. But Darius, too, was hurrying towards the coastal plain linking Cilicia-Syria.

Here, towards the end of 333, the decisive battle of Issus was fought between Alexander's 35,000 well-disciplined men and the overwhelming Persian cavalry of 30,000 and 70,000 foot, composed of Persians and Greek mercenaries. Darius was so confident of victory that he had brought his mother and his wife and family to witness it. In the event his troops were overcome by the Macedonian onslaught and he himself had to desert his remaining military forces and flee from

Figure 40. Oxus Treasure. Gold armlet from the Oxus Treasure. The ends are decorated with horned griffins, a popular motif in Achaemenian art. The armlets were inlaid with coloured stones, almost all of which are now missing. 5th-4th century BC. Ht. 12.3 cm. Courtesy, Trustees of the British Museum.

the battlefield in his war chariot, which he soon abandoned in favour of his horse,

The Macedonians then descended on Darius' headquarters in Damascus, where they found the immensely valuable Persian baggage-train, as well as the royal family: the queen, the queenmother and the royal children, who were treated as befitted their rank. They also found and took prisoner the Athenian and Spartan ambassadors who were there to seek a treaty of mutual assistance to rid the Persians and themselves of their Macedonian enemy.

Continuing his march southwards, Alexander entered the open, welcoming gates of Sidon. Tyre, which had extensive colonies and trading posts throughout the Mediterranean coastlands, withstood a siege of seven months before it was conquered. Its population was massacred or sold into slavery and the city was destroyed. The conquest of powerful and obstinately defended Tyre was probably the greatest military achievement of Alexander. Before the fall of Tyre Alexander received an embassy from Darius who offered him 10,000 talents for his family, together with peace terms: an alliance, his daughter's hand in marriage and all of Asia west of the Euphrates. Alexander refused. He wanted the whole of Asia, west as well as east of the Euphrates. He already held the land being offered and he did not need the father's consent to marry the daughter, if he so wished.

After a siege of two months against its courageous defenders, he took Gaza and massacred its population for their obstinacy. He then proceeded to Egypt. He was welcomed and fêted by the high priest in the temple of Amun at Memphis, and declared Pharaoh. The great city and the port of Alexandria was built: it captured the traditional important, and extensive trade of Tyre. Eventually, a great library was to give it the status of a centre of learning and heir to the Classical culture of Athens. There, Alexander founded his successor's dynasty – the Ptolemaic dynasty.

He allowed the Persian satrapal organisation to continue over the regions he conquered and this was to be his policy to an increasing extent, simply because his Macedonian and Greek followers were too small in numbers to wrestle with the administrative problems of the huge territories he was overruning. After a stay of four months, he departed from Egypt. In July 331, he rejoined his main army on the Euphrates. Both sides anticipated a decisive battle that would end the war.

The Macedonians fought their way across the Euphrates, where it turns towards Syria, and so over the Tigris to Gaugamela, the capital of the region, near Arbela (modern Erbil), where the main Persian force was encamped. It consisted of the *élite* Persian troops and the less disciplined but fierce forces of Sogdiana and Bactria, under their commander, Bessus, and levies of many peoples from the Caucasus to the frontiers of India. The cavalry of the large Nesaean breed of horses must have been a daunting sight against the much smaller, ordinary breeds of those times (including Alexander's own famous Bucephalos). There was a squadron of scythed chariots and the ground near Gaugamela had been smoothed for them. That was to be the battlefield, at the foot of the Assyrian mountains. The estimated numbers of combatants on the Persian side were 200,000 infantry, 40,000 cavalry and a contingent of elephants; while the Macedonians mustered only 40,000 infantry and 7,000 horse, but with a superior discipline, the new phalanx formation and a high moral. The combatants met for the third time. The battle as ever, was bravely fought by the king, his nobles and his famous bodyguard of the 10,000 'Immortals'. But the Persians were no match for the new military strategy and almost invincible, tight formation of the Macedonian phalanx which advanced upon a secretly demoralised king. Darius had lost so very much, besides his family. His queen had died: she had been given a royal burial by Alexander. In desperate sorrow, he had also lost his self-respect.

The combatants clashed amidst the thunder of racing chariots, galloping horses, the clash of spears and swords against shields and armour; a savage onslaught of shouting soldiery and screaming elephants. Then a brief, personal encounter between the furious Alexander, charging on his faithful Bucephalos and the disparate Darius and his charioteer in a final stand (as depicted on the dramatic mosaic from Pompeii, usually said to represent Issus (Naples Museum)). Darius turned and fled from the battlefield, in effect abdicating his kingship by doing so. Gaugamela was the last battle that the great House of Achaemenes fought (October 331). Darius Codomannus was pursued, captured and murdered by his own cousin Bessus, satrap of Bactria, before Alexander could rescue him. Alexander then took off his cloak and wrapping it round the king's corpse, had it transported to Persepolis for a burial befitting a king. For details of these dramatic events, the reader must consult other sources, especially his biographers (see suggestions in the list of references at the end of the chapter).

The conqueror entered Babylon in triumph. Young and energetic, intelligent and successful, the populace welcomed him with song and dance and flowers. He respected their institutions, rebuilt the temple of Bel and retained their satrap. Arriving at the fabulous treasury, he rewarded all his men generously, giving even his mercenaries two months' extra pay. Thenceforth, he overflowed with munificence. Babylon received its original status which it had forfeited under Xerxes.

After a month of rest and recreation for all, he set out, with the great train of Babylonian treasure, for Susa, the capital, which had capitulated after Gaugamela. There, in store, was to be found the fabulous riches and gold of the Persian

Empire. The value of the ingots of gold and silver has been estimated at about £15,000,000 (1931 values). He stayed in Susa briefly to assess his gigantic acquisitions made in such a short time. He decided on an idealistic (and, realistically, necessary) cooperation of nations. The huge Empire could not be goverened by a handful of Macedonians and Greeks. Mixed marriages were encouraged; he himself married Darius' daughter, as well as (later) a Bactrian princess.

To reach Persepolis he defeated a Persian force at the narrow pass of the Persian Gate and overran the rich city so quickly that the Persian garrison could not plunder its treasure before his arrival (Arrian III.18). According to Plutarch (Alexander 37) and Strabo (XV.iii.9) this amounted to 40,000 (Attic) talents. Arrian continues: 'he burnt the palace of Persian kings . . . against the advice of (his second in command) Parmenion, who urged him to spare it . . . chiefly because it was hardly wise to destroy what was now his own property, and because he would alienate the Asians.' Alexander replied that he wished to punish the Persians for their invasion of Greece and the burning of Athens (Arrian III.19). In Arrian's view, this was a bad policy, especially as 'it would hardly be considered as punishment for Persians long since dead and gone.' Plutarch (Alexander 38) and Diodorus (17-72) write that the burning was a challenge to Alexander by Thaïs, the Athenian courtesan, at a drinking party. There are a number of versions for the reasons of that wanton destruction of an architecturally beautiful palace of great historical interest, but this seems to be the one that is generally accepted on both sides.

Then, he went on to seize Bactria and to fight a successful war in the Punjab (327). Eventually, he sailed down the Indus and after many adventures with which we cannot be concerned here he returned to Babylon. He died from an unknown disease, contracted, it is said, while swimming in the Euphrates (323). Thus ends the history of the Persian Empire; a tiny glimpse, its momentary statement as represented here, matching the same treatment given to the histories of the previous civilizations in this sketch of the Ancient History of the Near East.

In a brief recapitulation and assessment of their achievements, the Persians must firstly be given the credit for uniting all the Iranian peoples in the foothills and valleys of the Zagros mountains, the Medes being by far the most important of them. Eventually, they demonstrated an exceptional administrative ability and political diplomacy, in sustaining an empire larger and more complex than any other before it. It included all the peoples between the Aegean and Syria in the west, and Bactria and the Indian frontiers in the east; the Caucasus in the north and the Persian Gulf and Egypt in the south, an administrative feat never before achieved.

The Persian wars were peripheral, mainly with the Greeks and the Egyptians, far to the west of Susa and the Euphrates. Hence architecture, art and commerce, literature and science and cultural development generally were taken up from their oriental predecessors and continued uninterrupted within the Persian Empire. The cultural wealth of the most ancient east flowed to all parts of the empire making its mark in Ionia, in Greece itself and even in Egypt. The Persians, inheritors of the most ancient Babylonian cultural legacies, must have introduced certain as the Indus Valley (witnesses of trading relations) which had continued between the subcontinent and the Persian Gulf from the most ancient times.[14]

They also extended the underground irrigation system, called qanat, which they inherited from Assyria, thus increasing the productivity of large regions to feed the ever-growing population. They encouraged the development of science, inherited from Babylon. Its advanced nature might be illustrated by the fact that Babylonia's astronomers (c. 500 BC), could calculate the regular lunar eclipses more accurately than Copernicus;[15] Cidenas of Sippar, a Babylonian astronomer, discovered the precession of the equinoxes, as early as c. 340 BC, although the discovery of that phenomenon is attributed to Hipparchus of Nicaea (c. 150 BC).

> The passage of 70 years brings about a shift of one degree in the equinoctial sun in the zodiacal belt. A complete rotation is a matter of about 26,000 years.[16]

The Persians themselves imaginatively adopted the western Aramaic alphabet, and made that language universal for the whole of their Empire. It must have been the most cohesive factor in that vast region. They also incorporated into their Zoroastrian religion the Semitic idea of survival after death in some form, yet another powerful unifying factor of the largely Semitic peoples west of the Persian home frontiers.

THE LAWS and Texts of Darius are inscribed on the cliff-face at Behistun. Fragments have been found on tablets or papyri in some of the main centres of the Empire – at Susa, Persepolis, Naqsh-i-Rustam, Elephantine. This last was translated into Aramaic, for the benefit of the large number of Jewish mercenaries garrisoned in Egypt. They have parallels in the Code of Hammurabi, which seems to have served as the inspiration for Darius' counsellors who drew up the laws (as, seemingly, it had influenced the Jews). The Inscriptions often refer to Ahura-Mazda, the great God of the monotheistic Darius (see below, section on Religion), in whose name the laws were promulgated. They begin by asserting Darius's royal lineage, as a god-given status, thus establishing his credentials:

> A great god is Ahura-Mazda, who created this earth, who created yonder sky, who created man, who created happiness for man, who made Darius king of many, one lord of many. (Ahura-Mazda: Xerxes refers to 'Ormuzd', another form of Mazda, on an inscription quoted above).
>
> I am Darius the Great King, King of Kings, King of countries containing all kinds of men, King in this great earth far and wide, son of Hystaspes, an Achaemenian, a Persian, son of a Persian, an Aryan, having Aryan linage.
>
> Saith Darius the King: Much which was ill-done, that I made good. Provinces were in commotion; one man was smiting the other. The following I brought about by the favour of Ahura-Mazda, that the one does not smite the other at all, each one is in his place. My law – of that they feel fear, so that the stronger does not smite nor destroy the weak.
>
> Saith Darius the King: May Ahura-Mazda bear me aid . . and may he protect this country (and its people) from a hostile army, from famine, from the Lie (Darkness, Ill-fortune). Upon this country may there not come an army, nor famine nor the Lie.[17]

Hammurabi's version is that he rules in the name and by order of the gods:

> At that time, Anu and Enlil named me, Hammurabi, the exalted prince, the worshipper of the gods, to cause righteousness to prevail in the land, to destroy the wicked and the evil, to prevent the strong from injuring the weak, and to further the welfare of the people.[18]

These are some clauses of the laws which show similarities between the Persian and the most ancient Babylonian laws. First and perhaps most important of all, in both cases: 'that the king's exalted and mighty position is in accordance with the will of the gods; that the strong shall not smite the weak, or take advantage of the widow and the deprived'. In return, the king's subject is grateful for the safety and protection that the laws give him. A good Persian prays for the welfare of the king and for the whole of Persia and its people, among whom he is himself, of course, included.

There are similarities in laws governing marriage, the relationship between husband and wife, the status of women, commercial transactions, reward and punishment, and so forth. The point being made is that the structure of great civilizations could only endure under powerful rulers, who are themselves inspired with confidence by God (the gods) whose laws perpetuate those disciplines of the fundamental institutions of society which are valid for all time.

These laws were enforced all over the Empire by the king's judges, whose integrity was guaranteed by the king himself. However, some judges can be corrupted. In one such case, as told by Herodotus (V.25), the wicked judge 'who had taken money to give an unrighteous sentence, was slain and flayed, his skin was cut into strips and stretched across the seat of the throne whereon he had been wont to sit when he heard causes'. This was in the time of Cambyses; in later times the Persians seem to have flayed their criminals alive.

RELIGION: Religion, of course, could be categorised as a branch of philosophy – the love of knowledge; the difference between intellectually argued temporal conclusions on the one hand and beliefs and convictions described as 'faith' on the other hand, rooted into us in the course of our upbringing, or sometimes resulting purely from personal experiences, which do not apply universally. Be it through philosophical interpretation or as a result of Belief, each one's personal Knowledge is imminent within one's psyche and often incomprehensible to others.

Certain individuals, as a result of their convictions and the faith they have in the integrity of their personal experiences, become powerful teachers and persuade others to accept what they themselves know to be the Truth, in the religious sense. For example, that God is Good, and that Evil exists only to demonstrate the beauty and power of the Good, which ultimately prevails. It could be argued that the goal of every religious devotee is to attain the greatest proximity, indeed, to be embraced and absorbed into the Spirit which is characterised as God or the Good.

All religions, including the 'primitive' ones, might be described in such terms. The tortuousness of the path to that destination is in direct proportion to the moral integrity of society – the higher the intelligence expressed in morality, the simpler is the path approaching God, or the Great, all-pervasive Universal Spirit; the more civilized (caring and just) is a community, the fewer are the gods or 'saintly' intermederies, and the less tortuous is the path leading to God. This might be described as a synthesis, perhaps a simplistic philosophy which might be accepted or rejected by the reader, according to his own convictions.

These introductory observations are necessary in the context of Achaemenid Persia, a great empire, consisting of many peoples with their numerous gods, descended from gods of the earliest times. The period overlapping the seventh and sixth centuries BC could be described as a watershed of great intellectual changes, comparable perhaps to the physical changes of the 13th-12th centuries BC (Ch. 8, *The Sea Peoples*). It produced within 50 years of each other, Buddha, Zoroaster and Confucius; the first two with spiritual convictions and the third offering temporal rules of behaviour, which are still honoured in China. The political turmoil of the seventh and sixth centuries BC, when the last of the most ancient Semitic civilizations, Assyria, gave place to the new, Aryan Persian Empire, encouraged safe travel and exchange of ideas between east and west, and the westwards emigration of the oriental and Ionian intellectuals to Athens, in response to the invitations of Pericles in the fifth century BC.

The Persian Great Kings had somehow to integrate the teachings of Zoroaster into the existing religions. Zoroaster was probably a Bactrian, close to India, who lived, perhaps, in the seventh century BC and, if so, a contemporary of Buddha. In his teachings, Zoroaster seems to amalgamate the ancient beliefs and the worship of a plurality of good spirits, called Ahuras, acolytes of the One Supreme Being, Ahura-Mazda (Creator of the Universe), the Ormuzd of the modern Parsees. He set out to reform the older religions with their demons – the daevas – the (nature) gods, the worship of which had been perpetuated by the Magian priests (the Fire-priests).

However, it is not possible to speak of the 'Good' or the 'Right' without a standard by which to measure it. Good or Right would be meaningless without the presence of 'Evil' or the 'Lie'. Zoroaster offered two original Causes, the Good Mind (Vohu Manö) and the Bad Mind (Akem Manö), and these twin Causes, as a single spirit are, he taught, all-pervasive. In this sense, therefore, Zoroastrian teaching is monotheistic.

It is not easy for the weak, worldly man to understand and accept such an apparently dual concept as monotheistic, surrounded as he seems to be by so much Evil as well as some Good. How can two such opposites live in the same house? The philosopher does not find it too difficult to accept that concept, for he has but to look within himself to find them both housed together. But others must have symbols of the Good (the Sun and Fire – Ahura-mazda (Light) and separately, that of Evil (Darkness – Ahriman). Therefore, Zoroaster's teaching appears to be dualistic; and both the god of Good and that of Evil must be worshipped and propitiated in their own right. That vulgar idea of dualism degenerates further by symbolising and, indeed, deifying other aspects of life. The old Magian form of fire-worshipping, therefore, continued with multifarious gods representing one or other aspect of the universe – the sun, the sky, the moon, the stars and so forth.

Zoroaster's legendary doctrines are written in the Avesta, the Persian scriptures. The only parts which are recognised by scholars as the work of Zoroaster himself or of his times, are the Metrical hymns in his Book, known as the Gathas, in a distinct dialect. The original version of Zoroastrianism, which the Achaemenids adopted, had also degenerated to the intellectual level of ordinary folk by the time of Artaxerxes II (404-359).[19] Herodotus, who died c. 400, writes (I.131-140):

> Their custom is to ascend the highest peaks of the mountains (ziggurats, towers) and offer sacrifices to Zeus (Ormuzd) calling the whole vault of sky, Zeus, and they sacrifice also to Sun, Moon, Earth, Fire, Water, and winds. To these alone they have sacrificed from the beginning.

Thus the Persian religion in the time of Herodotus retained much of the character of the earliest Aryan religions with their bloody rites and savage practices, but seemed to have forgotten the pure Zoroastrian monotheistic precepts.

Zoroaster, in contrast to the version given by Herodotus, recognised no independent objects of worship in earth, water, fire and so forth, but rather, in a series of questions, which implied that Ahura-Mazda (i.e. the Wise Lord) himself controlled and directed the heavenly bodies and nature's annual cycles, as well as overseeing the perpetual battle, in the same house, between the Good, or Ahura, Light, and the Bad, or Ahriman, the Lie, Darkness; thus retaining the monotheistic nature of his teachings.

The result of the conflict between the daevas – the evil gods which Zoroaster set out to expung, – 'infected the world of men'. Zoroaster pointed the way out of the dilemma in which man found himself, by showing the way to attain the Right (Ahura-Mazda) and to destroy the Lie or the evil spirits of the ancient daevas. Victory is certain, for Ahura-Mazda, and his followers will attain blessing and delight, while the Lie and its adherents – those who have rejected Ahura-Mazda – will receive cruel torment. In immortality shall the soul of the righteous be joyful, in perpetuity shall be the torment of the liars. Such is the way that monotheism – the Good – prevails and remains One, while the Bad is relegated to oblivion – oblivion in this case must mean resumption of the struggle, which again will bring more converts within the ethos of the Good. Evil is then an inferior power, within the greater power of the Good, by which it is always vanquished.[20]

Darius the Great, ruler of an empire consisting of peoples of many faiths, all polytheistic (even the Jews who believed in the power of Satan who is not always vanquished (as in Zoroastrianism)), seems to have taken a diplomatic course in his religious expressions which would not alienate any of his subjects, while retaining his own belief in the monotheistic principles of Zoroaster. In his inscriptions at Behistun and elsewhere, he speaks of 'the other gods', but names only Ahura-Mazda.

That practice was followed by Xerxes and Artaxerxes I. 'Ahura-Mazda, who created heaven and earth, who created man, who defends my empire from evil'. But Artaxerxes II appeals to Ahura-Mazda, Anahita (the great mother-goddess) and Mitra (the unconquerable Sun and maintainer of compacts) to protect him, and,

> according to Berosus, he 'first taught the Persians the worship of the gods in human form and set up the image of Aphrodite-Anahitis at Babylon, Susa, Ecbatana, Damascus and Sardis.[20]

The Persian or Zoroastrian religion continued into the Second Persian Empire (the Arsacids and the Sassanians) and, while it was itself modified, it influenced the growth of Mithraism, which almost prevented Christianity from taking root, and to a larger or lesser extent

> forced the growth of ideas latent, but previously undeveloped in Judaism, and so affected the conditions under which the Christian religion came to birth; or again

what heretical ideas that gained currency in the earlier centuries of the Christian Church proceeded from Persia.[21]

Lastly, the above is intended to emphasise the great Achaemenian contribution to the foundations and the growth of western civilization through the transmission of their and their subjects' ideas between east and west – from India to Greece. While not in the least minimizing the enormous Hellenic contribution in the fields of every aspect of learning, these were built upon the foundations laid and initiatives offered by the earlier civilizations, culminating in those of Babylonia and Achaemenid Persia.

Notes

1. Singer Charles, *A Short History of Science*, Oxford University Press, 1941,p. 8.
2. Chahin M., *Some Legendary Kings of Armenia*, Third Edition, Taunton, U.K., 1993.
3. Layard Austen Henry, *Nineveh and Babylon*, John Murray, London, 1867, pp. 208-9.
4. *Ibid.*
5. Finlay Moses, quoted by Noel Annan on *Our Age*, London, 1990, p. 358.
6. Wells H.G., *The Outline of History*, London, 1937, p.292.
7. Fisher H.A.L. *A History of Europe*, Edward Arnold, London, p. 21.
8. Mitchell T.C. British Museum,Western Asiatic Antiquities Department.
9. *Ibid.*
10. Burney Charles, *From Village to Empire*, Phaidon, Oxford, 1977.
11. Fletcher Bannister, *History of Architecture*, Third Edition, Batsford, London, 1938, p. 61.
12. Singer Charles, *A Short History of Science*, *op. cit.*
13. Wheeler Mortimer, *The Indus Civilisation*, Cambridge University Press, 1968, p. 115.
14. Ghirshman R. *Iran*, Penquin, London, 1954, p. 204.
15. Hogben Lancelot, *Science for the Citizen*, George Allen & Unwin, London,1948, p. 64.
16. Ghirshman R., *Iran,op. cit.*, p. 153.
17. Harper Robert F., *The Code of Hammurabi*, col. I, II, 27-49, quoted by A.T. Olmstead in *History of the Persian Empire*, University of Chicago, 1948, p. 122.
18. G R Gray and M Cary, 'The Reign of Darius,' *CAH IV*. vii., 1969
19. *Ibid.*
20. *Ibid.*
21. *Ibid.*

Bibliography

Ref:
CAH I¹ = Cambridge Ancient History, Volume I part 1.
CAH II² = Cambridge Ancient History, volume II part 2.
AS = Anatolian Studies

Albright W.F. and Lambdin T.O., The Evidence of Language, *CAH II²*.
Albright W.H., 'The Armana letters from Palestine', *CAH II²*.
Aldred Cyril, 'Egypt, the Armana Period and the end of the Eighteenth Dynasty' *CAH II²*.
Annan Noel, *Our Age*, London, 1990.
Arrian *The Campaigns of Alexander the Great*, Penguin Classics, London, 1984.
Barnett R.D., 'Urartu', *CAH II¹*.
Barnett R.D., 'The Sea Peoples', *CAH II²*.
Breasted J. H., *Ancient Records of Egypt*, vol II, Chicago University Press, 1906.
Brummer Alex, *The Guardian*, newspaper, 4 May 1981.
Burney C., *From Village to Empire*, Phaidon, Oxford, 1977.
Burney C., and Lang D.M., *The Peoples of the Hills*, Weidenfeld and Nicolson, London, 1971.
Caskey John L., 'Greece, Crete and the Aegean Islands in the Early Bronze Age', *CAH II²*
Chahin M., *The Kingdom of Armenia*, Routledge, London, 1987.
Chahin M., *Some Legendary Kings of Armenia. Can they be Linked to Authentic History?* Third edition, London, 1993.
Cole Sonia, *The Neolithic Revolution*, British Museum Publications, London, 1970.
Cook J.M., *The Greeks in the Near East*, Thames & Hudson, London, 1962.
Cook J.M., *The Persian Empire*, JM Dent, London 1983.
Cottrell Leonard, *The Warrior Pharaohs*, John Evans, London 1968
Cottrell Leonard, *The Bull of Minos*, Evans, London, 1971.
Cottrell Leonard, *Reading the Past*, JM Dent & Son, London 1972.
Desborough V. R.d'A.,'The End of the Mycenaean Civilization and the Dark Ages', *CAH II²*.
Desroches-Noblecourt Christiane, *Tutankhamen*, The Connoisseur and Michael Joseph, London, 1969.

Deuel Leo, *Memoirs of Heinrich Schliemann*, Hutchinson, London, 1977.

Diakonoff Igor M., *Sale of Land in Presargonic Sumer*, Moscow, 1954.

Diakonoff Igor M., *The Prehistory of the Armenian People*, Caravan Books, New York, 1984.

Dower Margaret S., 'Syria Before 2200 BC', CAH II².

Dowsett C.J.F., *Historians of the Middle East*, Oxford, 1962.

Edwards I.E.S., *The Pyramids of Egypt*, Pelican, London, 1978.

Eisenfeldt O.,' Palestine in the Time of the Nineteenth Dynasty', CAH II².

Eisenfeldt O., 'The Hebrew Kingdom', CAH II².

Emery Walter B., *Archaic Egypt*, Penguin, London, 1961.

Erman and Blackman A., *Literature of the Ancient Egyptians*, Methuen, 1927.

Finlay M.I., *Early Greece*, Chatto and Windus, London, 1970.

Fisher H.A.L., *A History of Europe*, Edward Arnold, London.

Fletcher Bannister, *A History of Architecture*, BT Batsford, London, 1938.

Fox Robin Lane, *Alexander the Great*, Allen Lane, London, 1973.

Frankfort H., *The Art and Architecture of the Ancient Orient*, Harmondsworth, 1954.

Frazer James, *The Golden Bough*, Macmillan, London 1941.

Frye R.N., *The Heritage of Persia*, Weidenfeld and Nicholson, London, 1965.

Gadd C.J., 'The Dynasty of Agad and the Gutian Invasion', *CAH II²*.

Gardiner A.H., *Egypt of the Pharaohs*, Clarendon Press, Oxford, 1961.

Garstang John, *The Story of Jericho*, London 1940.

Goetze A., 'The Struggle for Domination of Syria, 1400-1300 BC', *CAH II²*.

Gray G.R. and Cary M., 'The Reign of Darius' *CAH IV.vii.*, 1969

Gulbekian E.V., 'Why did Herodotus think the Armenians were Phrygian Colonists', *AR*, Autumn 1991.

Gurney O.R., *The Hittites*, Pelican Books, 1976.

Hall A. H., *The Ancient History of the Near East*, Methuen, London, 1963.

Hawkes Jacquetta, *The First Great Civilizations*, Pelican, London 1977.

Hitti Phillip, K., *A Short History of Syria*, Macmillan, London, 1959.

Hodges Henry, *Technology in the Ancient World*, Allan Lane, London 1970.

Hogarth E.H., 'Lydia and Ionia', *CAH II¹*, 1960.

Hogben Lancelot, *Science for the Citizen*, George Allen & Unwin, London, 1948.

Hood Sinclair, *The Home of the Heroes*, Thames & Hudson, 1974.

James T.G.H., 'The Expulsion of the Hyksos', *CAH II¹*.

Jamme Albert, *The Guardian* newspaper, 4 May 1981.

Keller Werner, *The Bible as History*, Hodder & Stoughton, 1969.

Kenyon Kathleen, *Digging up Jericho*, Ernest Benn, 1957.

Kenyon Kathleen, *The Bible and Recent Archaeology*, British Museum Publications, 1978.

Khorenats'i Moses, *History of the Armenians*, tr., Robert W. Thompson, Harvard University Press, 1978.

Kupper J.R., 'Northern Mesopotamia and Syria', *CAH II¹*.

Labat René, 'Elam and Western Persia, c.1200-1000BC', *CAH II²*.

Landay Jerry M., *Silent Cities, Sacred Stones*, Weidenfeld and Nicolson, 1971.

Lang David M., *Armenia, Cradle of Civilization*, George Allen & Unwin, London,

1970.

Lauer J.P., *The Step Pyramid*, Service des Antiquités, Cairo.

Layard H.A., *Nineveh and Babylon*, John Murray, London, 1970.

Lloyd Seton, *The Art of the Ancient Near East*, Thames & Hudson, London, 1965.

Lloyd Seton, *Early Highland Peoples of Anatolia*, Thames & Hudson, London, 1967.

Lloyd Seton, *Ancient Turkey*, Guild Publishing, London, 1989.

Luckenbill D.D., *Ancient Records of Assyria and Babylon*, 1926-7.

Mackenzie D.A., *Egyptian Myth and Legend*, Gresham, 1913.

Macqueen G., 'Geography and History in Asia Minor in the Second Millennium BC', AS XI, 1968.

Mallowan Max E.L., *The Development of Cities from Al-'Ubaid to the End of Uruk*, CAH II.

Matz F., 'The Maturity of the Minoan Civilization', *CAH II¹*.

Mellaart James, *Earliest Civilizations of the Near East*, Thames & Hudson, London, 1965.

Mellaart James, 'Anatolian Trade with Europe and Anatolian Geography and Culture Provinces in the Late Bronze Age', *AS XVIII*, 1968.

Minns E.H., 'The Scythians and Northern Nomads', *CAH II¹*, 1960.

Mitchell T.C., *Sumerian Art Illustrated by objects from Ur and Al-'Ubaid*, British Museum Publications, 1969.

Mitchell T.C., *Western Asiatic Antiquities*, British Museum Publications.

Munn-Rankin J.M., 'Assyrian Military Power, 1300-1200 BC', *CAH II²*, 1975.

Oates David, 'Form and Function of Mesopotamian Temple Architecture', paper presented at the XXme rencontre archaeologique, Leiden, 1972, cf Archaeology 26, 1973.

Oates D. & J., *The Rise of Civilization*, Phaidon, Oxford, 1976.

Oates Joan, *Babylon*, Thames & Hudson, London, 1979.

Olmstead A.T., *History of the Persian Empire*, University of Chicago Press, 1948.

Paroda E., *Ancient Iran*, Methuen, London, 1965.

Piotrovsky Boris, *The Art of Urartu*, Evelyn Adams & Mackay, London, 1967.

Piotrovsky Boris, *The Ancient Civilization of Urartu*, London 1969.

Posner G., 'Syria and Palestine c.2160-1780 BC', CAH II².

Renault Mary, *Nature of Alexander*, Allen Lane, 1975.

Renfrew Colin, *Archaeology and Language*, Jonathan Cape, London, 1987.

Roux Georges, *Ancient Iraq*, Penguin, London, 1980.

Rowton M.B., 'Ancient Western Asia', CAH I¹.

Russell Bertrand, *A History of Western Philosophy*, George Allen & Unwin, 1948.

Saggs H.W.F., *The Greatness that was Babylon*, Sidgwick & Jackson, London, 1969.

Sandars N.K., *The Epic of Gilgamesh*, Penguin Books, 1982.

Sandars N.K. , *The Sea Peoples*, London, 1978.

Sewell Barbara, *Egypt Under the Pharaohs*, Evans Brothers, London, 1968.

Sinclair T.A., *Eastern Turkey*, Pindar Press, 1989.

Singer Charles, *A Short History of Science*, Oxford University Press, 1941.

Singer Itmar, 'Western Anatolia in the Thirteenth Century BC', *AS Vol. XXXIII*, 1983.

Smith Sidney, 'The Foundations of the Assyrian Empire', *CAH II¹*, 1960.

Smith Sidney, 'Sennacherib and Eshaddon', *CAH III*, 1960, p. 74.

Sollberger Edmond, *The Flood*, British Museum Publications, 1977.

Stubbings Frank H., 'The Recession of the Minoan Civilization', *CAH II¹*.

Taylour Lord Wm., *The Mycenaeans*, Thames & Hudson, London, 1964.

Tonybee Arnold, *Mankind and Mother Earth*, Oxford University Press 1976.

Tucker Anthony, *The Guardian* newspaper, 19 April 1985.

Watson Peter, *The Guardian* newspaper.

Wells H.G., *The Outline of History*, Cassell, London, 1920.

Woolley Leonard, *Mesopotamia and the Middle East*, Methuen, London, 1961.

Wheeler, Mortimer, *The Indus Civilization*, Cambridge University Press, 1968.

INDEX

Hittite(s), 12, 36, 37, 58, 60, 51, 70, 71, 73, 74-80, 82, 84, 87, 90, 100
Homer, 71, 80, 87
Homs, Lake, 58
Hor-Aha, Pharaoh, 63
Horemheb, 61
Horite, 74
Horses, 82, 85, 95, 96, 104
Hosea, 47
Hunger, Dr. Hermann, 34
Hurrian, 12, 60, 73, 74-7, 82, 91, 98
Hurri-Mitanian, *see* Mitanian
Hydarnes, 110, 121
Hyksos, 36, 41, 42, 56, 57, 63, 75, 77
Hystaspes, *see* Darius I.

Iliad, 70, 71, 86, 87
Imhotep, 53
Immortals, the 10,000, 121
Incense, 53, 56
India, 13, 14, 27, 76, 95, 99, 117, 119, 126
Indra, god, 76
Indus Civilisation, 14, 74
Indus, river, 125
Indo-Aryan, *see* Aryan
Indo-European, *see* Aryan
Ion -ia -ian -ic, 2, 69, 71, 73, 82, 102, 103, 111, 115, 117, 119, 120, 123
Ionic League, 112
Iran, 91, 108, 125
Iron, 5, 43, 82, 83, 88
Iron Age, 5, 82
Isaac, 40, 41, 46
Isaiah, 47
Ishmael, 41
Ishmaelites, 41, 95
Ishpuini, King, 14
Ishtar, (goddess), 76, 78, 91
Isin, 93
Isis, (goddess), 55
Israel -ites, 40-45, 63, 69, 88, 96, 99
Issus, 123
Italy, 84
Ivory, 53, 56
Izmir, *see* Smyrna

Jacob, 40, 41, 43, 46
Jamme, Father Albert, 44
Jehovah (Yahveh), 16, 39, 42, 44, 47
Jehu, 45, 96
Jeremiah, 47, 105, 106

Jericho, 3, 4, 43
Jeroboam II, King, 45
Jerusalem 43-46, 63, 96, 99, 105-6, 120
Jesus, 16, 39, 47
Jewish, 41
Jews, 31, 38-43, 45, 56-7, 95, 105, 106, 119
Jezebel, 45
Job, 47
Jordan, Trans-, 43, 45, 57
Jordan, R, 1
Joseph, 40-2, 56-7
Joshua, 40, 43, 63, 88
Josiah, King, 105
Judaism, 130
Judes, 43, 45, 96, 105, 106
Judges, 43

Kaaba, 42
Kadashman-Enlil, King, 37
Kadesh, 59, 62, 63, 76, 79
Kalhu, *see* Nimrud
Kanesh, 75, 76
Karnak, 59, 63
Karchemish, 76, 84, 92
Karkar, *see* Arapkha
Karum, 76
Karun, R, 1, 33, 74, 93
Kashka, 83
Kashtiliash, King, 91, 92
Kassites, 35-7, 74, 77, 87, 92, 93
Kenyon, Kathleen, 3
Kermanshah, 10, 109
Khafre, *see* Chefren
Khaldi, god, 102
Khanigalbat, *see* Syria
Khatti, 80, 82, 87, 100
Kheta, 58
Khorsabad, 102, 104
Khufu, *see* Cheops
Kimmerian(s), 88, 99-103
King, Leonard W, 110
Kirkuk, see Arapkha
Kish, city of, 18, 26
Kizzuwanda, 73, 82
Knossos, 64-8
Krakatoa, Volcano, 66
Kültepe, *see* Kanesh
Kurdistan, 76

Laban, 41